exploring the hand arts

GIRL SCOUTS OF THE U.S.A.
830 Third Avenue
New York, N. Y. 10022

This book was written by Corinne Murphy, Program Specialist in the Arts, Program Development Division. It was designed by Alvin Lustig and illustrated by Maurice Rawson.

contents

All these trust to their hands, and everyone is wise in his own art.

Without these a city is not built.

OLD TESTAMENT

to the leader

If you have the spirit of adventure and are willing to try new things, you can have great fun learning with your girls some of the joy of creative accomplishment. It is the purpose of this book to give you, the leader, enough material under one cover to feel confidence in working with your girls and to find enjoyment in the arts and crafts field.

Each chapter tell you a little about the basic material, the various possibilities, the tools and equipment needed, and some hints for projects. None of these projects requires expensive material, much time or storage space, or an expert knowledge of the arts. It is hoped that you will apply these basic techniques to whatever the girls want to make or to things they need for other troop activities. For example, if you learn the techniques for working in tin, you can make a tin-can stove, a lantern, or frying pan for camping. If the girls are interested in dramatics, read the section on papier-mâché. This craft can be used to make puppets, scenery, and masks. In the homemaking field you can combine textile painting with sewing or interior decoration. There are endless possibilities for interweaving arts and crafts with all other troop and camp activities. Some examples are given in this book.

1

Since this book is intended only to get you started, and the girls may want to know more about one particular subject, a rather complete bibliography has been included.

THE HAND ARTS AND THE GIRL SCOUT PROGRAM

The visual arts are one of the arts included in the total Girl Scout Program. Appropriate activity suggestions are included in the handbooks for each of the four age levels. The arts in Girl Scouting also include literature, dramatics, music, and dancing. All these arts are related to the cultural side of life. In combination or individually, they can give girls a rich experience in life and a chance to fulfill the basic human need for creative expression.

With the continuing industrial revolution leading us into a push-button age, there is no longer the physical necessity for creating something with our own hands, but the spiritual necessity still remains. To help fulfill that need, the arts are included in the Girl Scout program. No matter what badge or project a girl works on in the arts, she should receive some of the following benefits:

1. A release of tensions, a sense of accomplishment, and inner satisfaction.

2. Development of her appreciation and taste, including increased knowledge of the heritage of the arts.

3. Skills that can develop into lasting interests.

4. Development of her innate ability to think creatively and independently, and to formulate her own ideas.

In addition, Girl Scouting aims through program activities to help the girls to assume responsibility, to learn to work together, and to develop leadership. You ask, "How can visual arts activity do these things?" The answer is, "In many ways." Material and tools must be taken care of, put away carefully, used wisely. Who is responsible for these things? The girls. Suppose the troop is working on tooled leather and there are three sets of tools. It is obvious that the girls must share the tools and that while one patrol is working the rest must plan other activities—in short, they must learn to work as a group. And how do you manage to keep several patrols busy with different activities? Through the Court of Honor, of course. You plan with the patrol leaders. Teach them the techniques for tooling, a song, a dance, and they in turn help the other girls. The patrols can meet together at intervals to share their knowledge. With perhaps a troop committee member to help, four or five activities can proceed smoothly at one time. Refer to the Girl Scout Leaders' guides and the Girl Scout handbooks.

It is important to be able to distinguish what are arts and crafts and what are not. The areas of confusion are service projects, holiday crafts, and table decorations. All of these things must of necessity be similar and turned out quickly. They allow the child little or no chance to develop creative ability. For example, if the girls made one hundred nut cups as a service project, it is a mistake to feel they have had any experience in arts and crafts.

It is possible, of course, by working in a true art, such as woodcarving, to make a Christmas gift that can be called "arts and crafts." Some people feel that a girl must start and complete something in each meeting. This could not possibly be arts and crafts—merely "busy work." Anything worth while in the arts takes time and thought.

RESOURCES

There are many resources you can use to help you with your job. First and most obvious are books. Then there are films, filmstrips, and slides which may be rented or sometimes obtained free. Check with your local Girl Scout Council and your local library for books and videos on artists and art techniques.

People, too, may be used as resources. Perhaps some of the troop committee members can help you with certain projects. The lady up the street who does weaving, or your grandmother who hooks rugs, can be a resource person to you, teaching you something about her art. Consult your neighborhood chairman for program consultants. The program committee in a council usually keeps names of people in the community who are willing to talk about their special subjects. There may be artists, craftsmen, art teachers, or a Sunday painter who can teach you or come to your troop.

Use the consultants wisely. Before you ask someone to come to your troop, have a talk with her. Stress the importance of letting the girls start something simple and using their own ideas and designs. This is much better than the most illustrious lecture.

There are other natural resources in your community too. Perhaps it is a brick yard, woolen mill, shoe factory, metal works, lumberyard. These places always have scraps left and they are usually willing to give them to Girl Scouts. Some communities have natural clay, a quantity of reed or honeysuckle vine, or palmetto leaves. Use these natural resources very carefully so that you only take what is in excess and never mar the beauty of nature.

EVALUATION

When the year's fun and adventure are over, look for these evidences of growth. Do the girls show evidence of growth in:

1. Ability to express themselves.
2. Skill in handling tools.
3. Judgment in using forms, color, harmony, balance, textures, proportion.
4. Willingness to try new things and experiment.
5. Self-confidence in making decisions and long-term planning.
6. Self-reliance and independence in carrying a piece of work to its conclusion.
7. Appreciation of art forms and a growing sensitivity for good design and taste.
8. Cooperation with other children in group activities.

If the girls in your troop have accomplished some of these things through their art activities, then you are a grand success. You will have helped them in their spiritual, mental, and emotional growth as well as helping their creative ability.

Above all have they had fun!

design

Design is a magic word that is involved in everything made in arts and crafts. Perhaps you are saying, "But I can't design anything!" You would be surprised at how much of your life is design—the way you dress, the way you decorate your house, the way you set your table, even the way you arrange your closet. All these are forms of design.

Taste is something intangible and, therefore, difficult to describe; yet good taste should govern all design. Play the game on the next page and you will see there is an absolute in good taste and good design. This is based on the fundamental elements of fitness, proportion, balance, harmony, color, and rhythm.

HELPING THE GIRLS DESIGN

Only by creating their own designs can children realize the joy and satisfaction of art activities, and you will have to help them to achieve this. But remember that a child sees things differently at different times, and you should never try to force your standards on children. Because of the influence of coloring and copy books, you may find the girls dependent upon copying from books or from each

1a

1b

3a

3b

2b

4a

4b

2a

Choose the better design (See answers on page 104.)

other. This will be true at first, but by subtly leading them to create their own designs, you will witness a growth in ingenuity and creative thinking. This and the girls' sense of accomplishment will be your reward for the extra effort.

There are many ways to stimulate creativity. Try a bicycle or sketching trip, a discussion of a coming holiday or of the people and cultures of another country, or some flower or bird the girls have just discovered.

Children of Brownie age seem to be naturally expressive, but they need motivation. One method of doing this is the storytelling technique. As you read the story, the girls draw with crayon or paint a scene or character from the story. This method can also be used with clay.

Later on, have the girls listen to music and draw on fairly large pieces of paper what the sounds inspire or what the mood suggests. If some designs are nonobjective, point out parts that can be adapted to designs on wood, textiles, or leather. This may be done by darkening some lines and eliminating or adding others and filling in certain areas.

Girls nine to fourteen generally want to make tangible objects, but they, too, need help. The original stimulus may come from almost any source—the desire to work on a badge or a box of yarn donated to the troop. With the yarn, for example, point out how it can be used for weaving or needlepoint, for a hooked rug or embroidery. Help the girl decide what she needs for herself or would like to give as a gift. If it is a belt, it may be of needlepoint or one of several types of weaving. Ask her to think about what she will wear it with and to remember that harmony, color, and design are dependent on its use as well as on the material.

It is particularly important that the art program be diversified for this age. Give the girls a chance to explore and experiment with a variety of mediums, painting included. This is the age too when you can begin to weave art into interior decorating, good grooming, and fashion.

Senior Girl Scouts are ready to become really competent in an art. A girl of Senior Scout age is capable of handling tools adeptly and using more complicated techniques, of finding her own resources and learning more on her own. However, she still needs motivation to create something "her own." But remember, starting a new art at any age is just as difficult. A simple beginning is always safe.

CREATING A DESIGN

There are two basic ways to arrive at a design. You have some materials for which you need to find an appropriate use; or you have a definite object in mind that you want or need, and you have to find the suitable material for making it. Either approach can achieve beautiful and creative objects.

Suppose, for example, your troop has been given a box of leather scraps. First you would find out how and for what to use leather. It can be cut, sewed, glued, tooled, stamped, and dyed. One girl may make a strap for a notebook; another, a small leather lapel pin; another, a belt of different colored squares; another, a wall hanging of soft leather sections. It's entirely possible with the same basic materials to turn out a variety of items.

Here is an example of the second approach. Your troop has decided to make Christmas decorations for a community tree; then you search for appropriate materials. You can make decorations of paper, sections of egg cartons, heavy cellophane, colored straws, thin wood, plastic, copper or brass foil, and many other items. This book tells you how to use some of these materials. Let each girl collect a few scrap items she would like to work with. Put them all in a big box and then each girl can select a few and create her own designs at the meetings. The troop committee can help collect supplies, and may attend the meeting to help stimulate and work with the girls in experimenting.

THINGS TO MAKE

Try the following arts which are primarily for the sake of experimenting and learning to design. Be sure to point out the difference between experimentation and the finished design. Let the girls see that it's quite all right to experiment, decide they don't like a design, perhaps throw it away, and start on something else. You work on a design to completion only when it is really what you want to turn out.

Montage

This, a first step in designing, is the making of a new picture out of several pieces. Have the girls think about the kind of designs they want to make—a picture of an imaginary monster, a bouquet of flowers, a fruit arrangement, or just a scene. Have them cut heads, bodies, legs, arms of various animals or people, fruits and flowers from magazines and seed catalogs. Do all the cutting first, arrange the pictures on background paper, and then glue the pieces down when the design pleases. Discuss the finished pictures to see how the new designs were made and why some designs are better than others.

A similar art called decoupage has been used in many countries to create pictures and decorations for furniture and trays.

If one or two of the girls arrive at a really good picture, they might try mounting or framing it.

Collage

This art is similar to montage but goes a step further into dimension and texture. Have the girls collect various pieces of colored paper, sandpaper, corrugated paper, cellophane, pieces of fabric, wire screening, paper clips, rubber bands, tin foil, feathers, toothpicks, rope, string, colored yarns, tape, etc. In other words, just a miscellaneous collection of items. Have sheets of paper or cardboard and glue on hand. The best way to work with these articles is to have them all together in a large flat box in front of the girls. They choose items that appeal to them, arrange a composition, and glue it down. Help them to include texture and interesting color combinations, and to arrive at a pleasing balance. The result may be just lines, colors, and shapes; it may represent an illustration for a story; or it may be animals or scenes. Take time to set all designs up and let the girls discuss which ones they like best and why. This evaluation helps them to see the principles involved in good design.

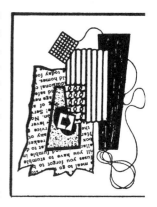

Mobiles

Mobiles are designs that hang in space, shifting with each air current to create new and fascinating designs in motion and shadow. There can be a great deal of genuine fun and release of tension in making a mobile. You can use practically any material—wood dowels, thin pieces of veneer, wire, thin metal pieces, cellophane, construction

paper, and miscellaneous items such as Christmas balls, ping-pong or small rubber balls, hatpins, a tiny bell for sound as well as movement. The principle is to suspend the hanging objects in such perfect balance that the design moves with every shift in air current. Therefore, the items cannot be too heavy. The mobile is hung with black thread and each item is hung with black thread or thin wire to give the illusion of floating in space. Your design may be composed within a circle, square, or any geometric form, or may be composed of several sizes of dowel or wire with items hanging from them. You may have a general theme to begin with or you may just be inspired by what is on hand.

These arts are presented here as experimental techniques to help the child learn to design. However, the collage and mobile are very definitely contemporary art forms. The artist Alexander Calder designs mobile decoration for thousands of dollars and the mobile is widely used in advertising. The collage takes its place in galleries beside more traditional art forms. These art forms can be used to advantage with older girls to create really special decoration.

You will be able to pick other experimental techniques out of the chapters to suit individuals, such as creative embroidery, crayon etching, or just the simple technique of using wet colored chalk on paper. Some children are sensitive to color, others to texture, some are good with tools, some have greater powers of appreciation. Only the rare child has everything but every child has something.

ADAPTING A DESIGN

The best way to design something of your own is to get your inspiration from nature, the way people walk and dance, lights and shadows, or the various objects around you. For craft work, primitive or peasant art is an excellent source for inspiration for here design is seldom ill used. The important thing is that you do not represent what you see exactly as you see it, but adapt certain lines that are characteristic and work out a design in this manner.

This is the way that folk art is designed. The people who do these folk designs are not artists, just people like you who express what they see in design. The illustration

10

Adapting a design

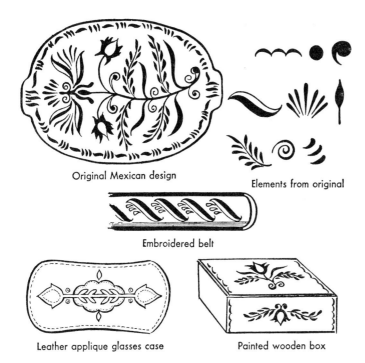

Original Mexican design

Elements from original

Embroidered belt

Leather applique glasses case

Painted wooden box

on this page will show you clearly how to use folk art designs as source material. Notice how the original design was changed to be appropriate to each different medium. The design is not copied—the idea or single motif is taken to create new designs. As you use source material in this way, you will find that more and more you can depart from the original and put your own personality into the work.

Encourage a child never to copy a design directly. It will give her *none* of the spiritual gifts that art should give. You can explain to the girls how doing their own work is related to the Girl Scout Promise and Laws. For example, it would not be honest to say, "I made this," if the design was copied or the article assembled from a ready-made kit. This is part of what is meant by "the Girl Scout program is more than activities."

11

paper

Paper is inexpensive, yet it offers untold possibilities for starting a creative adventure. Have you ever thought of all the different kinds of paper that exist? There are the practical papers—newsprint, corrugated paper, sandpaper, shelf paper. There are the art papers—charcoal, watercolor, and rice paper. There are the fancy papers—metallic paper, wallpaper, wrapping paper, and fascinating Japanese papers with leaves embedded in them. Some of your girls may enjoy collecting different kinds of paper.

At a troop meeting the girls could cut and arrange pieces of some of their paper in patterns or designs, then glue them down on a plain piece of paper. It's a good way for them to start learning about proportion, balance, color, and texture, and it is a type of collage. Think of all the ways paper can be handled. You can staple and glue it, twist and coil it, cut and fringe it. You can decorate it with paintings or prints and use it for bookbinding or covering objects. Paper is a first-rate medium through which children can discover their own creative abilities. They can really let their imaginations run wild. The rules are few, the possibilities unlimited. There are many suggestions in this chapter that will start to develop a child's creative imagination and others that can help older girls acquire real skills.

Paper, like all the art mediums, can be related to the total Girl Scout program. For example, you can understand other people so much better if you know a little about their culture and their folk art. Through the art of paper-cutting you can learn about the Middle European countries and also about our own early settlers who did beautiful lacy paper-cuttings representative of their life. Find out about the lovely paper-covered objects made in Italy. Learn about the special holidays and fiestas for which the Mexicans make papier-mâché masks. Did you know the children make identical masks for themselves and for their dolls?

There is plenty of room for service too. Papier-mâché penny banks or puppets might be welcomed in a children's hospital ward. And, with a little stimulation, the troop can go from papier-mâché to dramatics.

Remember, the girls are to use only the best designs. Suzie may make ten paper-cuttings but only one may be good enough to keep. Don't judge by your own standards. Help her to set standards for herself, to persevere, and to feel the satisfaction of creating something really beautiful and all her own.

DECORATING PAPER

The girls may have a special project in mind that calls for decorating paper. It may be a Christmas card, bookplate, or a paper to make a bookbinding, portfolio cover, or a wrapping for a special gift. Perhaps they just want to use paper to create a picture. The kind of drawing or painting will determine the kind of paper to use. Your art supply dealer can help decide the type needed. In addition to the following methods of decorating paper, you will find others in the chapter on prints.

Marbleizing

Marbleized paper is excellent for book covers or linings. It can also be used to cover boxes and other objects.

You will need: size, shallow tray, oil colors or printing inks, turpentine, water, stick or feather, paper that is not too absorbent, newspapers.

Dissolve about 2 ounces of powdered size (obtainable at hardware stores, or make your own, see page 67) in 1 pint of boiling water. Stir until it is completely dissolved. Pour the mixture into a shallow tray and add about 5

13

pints of water. If the tray is too small to hold as much as this, use smaller amounts in proportion.

In separate containers, mix the desired oil colors or printing inks with turpentine to the consistency of thick cream. Test by dropping a spot of color on the pan of size. If it sinks, it is too thick; if it spreads too much, it is too thin.

When it is ready, drop spots of color (one color or different colors) all over the size. Work the color into patterns of swirls or wavy lines by stirring or raking the size with a small stick or feathers.

Holding the paper to be marbled (cut to the size of the tray) by opposite corners, lower it carefully onto the size, seeing that all parts of the paper come in contact with the liquid.

Lift it carefully and place it right side up on newspaper to dry.

Crayon etching

If you want to create an effective picture or book cover, you will be delighted with this experiment which is related to the scratchboard technique.

You will need: cardboard (such as 2-ply Bristol board) or fairly heavy paper, crayons, black India ink, brush, sharp instrument, clear shellac, newspapers.

Take a smooth, fairly heavy paper (such as 2-ply Bristol board). Coat the surface with crayon with one color or several colors in a pattern—no two colors on top of each other. Build up the crayon by going over the paper lightly several times rather than once with heavy strokes. Cover the whole with a coat of black India ink. When it is thoroughly dry, scratch a design with any sharp-pointed instrument—a nail, hatpin, or jackknife. A coat of shellac or plastic spray over the finished product protects it from further scratches.

Finger painting

Although finger painting isn't strictly a craft, it is a good way to have fun and experiment with color and design. You can buy finger paints already made or make your own with this recipe.

2 cups laundry starch	1 cup soap flakes
1 cup boiling water	

Mix the starch with cold water to make a creamy paste. Add boiling water and stir over a low flame until the mixture is clear. Let it cool slightly and stir in soap flakes. Keep in a covered jar. The color is added later.

You will need: finger paints, finger-paint paper or washable shelf paper, pan of water, oilcloth.

Hold the sheet of paper by one side and draw it slowly through the pan of water until it is wet through. Allow the surplus water to roll off. Lay it flat, glossy side up, on a table covered with oilcloth. Smooth the paper and put a dab of the starch medium on it. Add poster paint color (purchased finger paints are already colored) and go to it with fingers, hands, arms, and elbows. Be sure you are well covered with a smock or apron. Try one-color designs first, then try two-color designs, letting the first color set before adding the second. You may use your designs to cover a wastebasket, lampshade, or to make a small cardboard screen, a telephone book cover, or a filing case. Give it a coat of shellac as a protective covering.

THINGS TO MAKE

Cut paper

One of the most beautiful arts using paper is the old folk art of cut-paper decoration which is found in many countries. Some of these may be found in museums and antique shops.

You will need: strong, pliable paper for cutting, tissue paper, sharp-pointed scissors (when the girls become more skillful they may use a single-edge razor blade or sharp stencil knife), Higgins vegetable glue, pencil, soft clean cloth, and a board to work on.

One way to start is to try the tissue paper flags used in many countries for decoration. For these you need several colors of tissue and a dime-store Chinese matchstick table

mat. Take a piece of tissue the size you wish for your finished flag, fold it several times, and cut a design. Only by experimenting will you discover the different effects you can achieve. When a flag satisfies you, take a stick from the mat, coat one side or edge of it with glue, and attach the flag. You can hang it with thin gold cord.

For other cut-paper designs you need strong pliable paper that does not crack when bent. Some of the plain-colored wrapping papers are fine, especially the heavy ones that come in luminous colors and silver and gold. You will also need a mounting paper which can be any heavy paper or cardboard. The usual procedure is to mount a white cutout on black background, but gold and silver are often used and are very effective. Start simply, perhaps just by folding and cutting little men and women in a row holding hands, then try something more difficult as shown. You may want to sketch your cutting lines on the wrong side at first, but when you have mastered the art, free cuts are best. Designs inspired by other countries are shown on these pages.

Germany

India

To glue your finished work to the backing, place your design right side down on the tissue paper and apply the glue evenly over the entire back with brush, finger, or cloth. Pick it all up and place it on the background. Rub gently with the cloth and carefully peel off the tissue paper. Then rub with the cloth from the center of the design out to the edges to wipe off any excess glue. If you do not cover your design with glass, coat it with a clear plastic spray or shellac.

Cut-paper designs can be mounted and framed and used simply as decoration. You can also use the designs for any number of other objects. They can be mounted on wooden book ends, wastebaskets, trays, on a book cover, boxes, and many other objects.

Paper coverings

There are many articles that can be attractively covered with paper that you have decorated yourself or have bought already decorated. Italian artists have produced many fine objects using decorative papers. Choose a paper with a design in good proportion to the article you are covering.

17

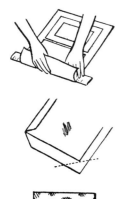

You will need: the object to be covered, the paper or fabric to cover it, scissors, Higgins glue, black India ink, watercolors and brush, shellac and alcohol, wax paper, soft cloth, ruler, table knife.

Carefully measure the object to be covered and draw its outline with a ruler on the back of your paper, again measuring carefully. Draw the table knife along the lines to be cut without cutting through the paper. Experiment first on a scrap piece to determine pressure. Fold the straight edges over the ruler and miter all corners. (See illustration.) Dampen the paper and object slightly and apply paste to the object. Smooth your work by flattening and pressing out excess moisture from the inside to the edges with a rolling pin or soft cloth. While you are working on one part, you can prevent the paper from sticking to the other parts if you put wax paper between paper and the object. Remove the wax paper as you go along. Cover the finished article with wax paper and put it under a weight to dry. You may decide an accent of black India ink or watercolor would pep up the design. Use it sparingly. Pieces that will be handled need a coat of shellac to protect them.

Paper sculpture

Paper sculpture is the art of manipulating paper into a three-dimensional effect.

You will need: strong but pliable paper, scissors, cellophane, tape, stapler.

First decide on the design, size, and background for the sculpture. Select your paper according to the desired effect. Experimentation and imagination are your real guides. Your design should stand away from the background or be free standing. The picture opposite shows you some suggestions for joining pieces and some techniques for additional effects such as curling paper with scissors, fringing, and cutting spirals from circles. In addition to designs that go against a background and the free-standing designs, there are several ways of twisting and cutting paper to make handsome Christmas decorations or mobiles. These are shown on page 10. For effect in your designs you can use such miscellaneous items as wooden beads, bits of fabric, braid trimmings, copper foil.

The designs on a background can be effectively used for wall decoration, for posters, for holiday decorations on doors, etc. You may also use such paper sculpture as background for small stages for puppet or marionette shows. The free-standing sculpture can be used as a decorative object the year round or for holiday decoration on a table or mantel.

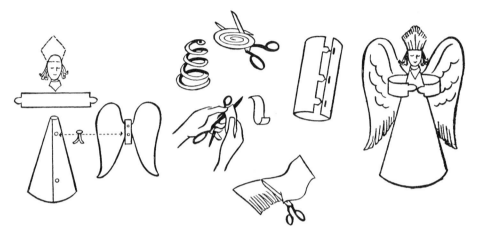

Papier-mâché

People who work with papier-mâché have their favorite method of using it. Two of the methods are given below so that you may choose the one you like best. The first is perhaps the easier to handle if you're a beginner.

You will need: newspaper and paper toweling, flour or wheat paste (wallpaper paste) or starch, Higgins glue, scissors, covering for table, string, grease, tempera paint and brush, shellac, alcohol to clean brush, gummed tape, buttons, beads, scraps of string and wire.

When creating your object, you need something to use as a mold or base. You can make a puppet head, mask, animal, bowl, tray, or penny bank. For a puppet head, make your mold from crushed paper with string tied around to keep it firm, or use a light bulb or a head modeled in clay; for a mask, mold over a rounded shape such as a gallon bottle, clay form, or paper plate; for an animal, roll coils of paper and tie with a string. If you wish to make fruit or penny bank, use a greased apple or orange for a mold. When the covering is dry, cut the mold in two and put back together with pieces of papier-mâché.

19

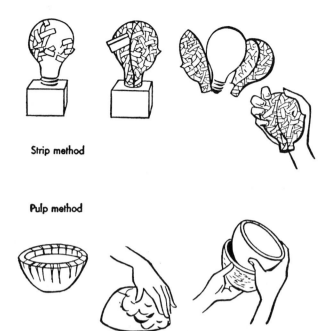

Strip method

Pulp method

You can mold a bowl or tray from an actual bowl or tray. Cover the outside with grease or wax paper and then apply pulp. When pulp hardens, lift out your mold.

STRIP METHOD. Tear pieces of paper into 1- or 2-inch squares or strips 1-inch wide, dip in paste, and cover your mold or form by overlapping the paper pieces.

PULP METHOD. Soak small pieces of paper in warm water until soft, mix in a small amount of flour paste or laundry starch that has been cooked until creamy. The paper will disintegrate. Take a handful of the pulp, squeeze out most of the liquid, and put an even layer of the pulp over your mold.

To build up areas in your design (a mask, for example), fasten on crumpled wads for nose and eyebrows before putting on layers. Put as many layers over your mold as is necessary to make it firm (usually 6 to 8 layers will do). A final layer of paper-toweling strips makes a good finish on which to paint. Plaster of Paris sprinkled lightly between layers, or paper strips dipped in starch, makes a firmer finished product. Let your work dry thoroughly. This may take two or three days. Put it near a warm or sunny place if possible, because fast drying is best. Remove from mold, trim edges, sand lightly to smooth the surface, then paint. Cover it with a protective coat of shellac after the paint dries. If you are making a mask or fanciful animal, add trimmings of feathers or sequins while

20

the shellac is sticky. Trimmings can also be stapled, sewed, or pasted on.

Gesso and paper

Gesso is a powder that is mixed with water and used to prepare artists' canvas for painting. You can purchase it in art supply stores, 2 pounds for about $1.25, which is enough for 10 or 12 projects. When painted in several layers over a paper or cardboard base, it hardens until it becomes like papier-mâché. It is inexpensive, easy to handle, and produces a good-looking result. It is not as versatile as papier-mâché, but is excellent for trays or boxes.

You will need: paper plates or trays (heavy paper meat market containers), cardboard boxes, gesso, enamel, shellac, alcohol to clean brush, wide brush, small brush, sandpaper, knife or razor blade, stove or hotplate.

Mix gesso in a glass jar according to the directions on the can. (Use 2 pounds to 1 quart of water or ½ pound to a little less than ½ pint of water.) Place jar in a pan of cold water and bring water to a boil, then simmer to keep warm while you work. It is not necessary to make a new batch each time, but it is necessary to reheat it, adding a little water as gesso tends to thicken.

Coat both sides of plates or trays, pressing two together to make extra firm; or if you are using one, coat one side, dry, then coat the other side. Put a weight in the bottom and let tray dry overnight. Be sure to wash the brush immediately after each use.

When covering a box, cover the inside and out first with a coat of shellac to make it firmer. So that the cover will fit tightly, apply gesso only to the inside rim of the bottom and the outside rim of the top.

After it dries completely, bevel the edges with a sharp knife or safety razor blade. Apply another coat of gesso, carefully filling all cracks and chinks.

Apply as many coats of gesso as necessary, usually about 4, to produce the desired rigidity. Let dry between each coat. Be careful to apply gesso smoothly because sanding it smooth afterward is more difficult. Sand lightly after the last coat is dry.

Apply several coats of enamel, sandpapering lightly between coats, and decorate by painting or adding objects if you wish. Finish with a protective coat of shellac.

21

prints

Prints are fun. You can start with many common things —copper scouring pads, corks, shells, sticks—and they can be used for many things—posters, costumes, greeting cards, bookplates, leaf prints, window curtains. From this short list of possible uses, you can see how prints may be related to the other fields of interest and to service projects. But remember, only those prints that incorporate the principles of good design should be used for the finished article.

KINDS OF PRINTS

A print is an impression or imprint made from a plate, block, or stone on which a design has been etched, engraved, cut, or otherwise marked on by the artist. There are roughly three classes of prints.

1. Those in which the design is depressed—intaglio prints. They are produced by cutting or etching what is to be printed into a metal plate. The ink remains in the hollowed-out lines. Dampened paper is laid over the plate, heavy pressure is applied which forces the paper into the ink-filled lines, producing the print. Etchings, dry points, mezzotints, and aquatints come in this class.

2. Those with a design that is raised—relief prints. They are obtained by cutting away all the surface not to

22

be printed, leaving the lines of the design raised. When an ink roller is passed over the surface, the ink adheres only to the raised lines. Prints are then made by pressing the block on paper or fabric. Block prints come under this class.

3. Those with the design on a flat surface—planographs.

a. Lithograph—printed from a stone on which the design is drawn in a grease crayon. When inked, only the areas drawn in crayon will take the ink. Well-known print-makers are Goya, Daumier, Delacroix, Ingres, Currier and Ives, and George Bellows. Museums and libraries will acquaint you with their work. The art of lithography began about 1796.

b. Monotype—printed by covering the plate with ink and rubbing the design into the wet ink with a finger, brush, or stick. Only one impression can be made by this method, which began in the seventeenth century.

The block print is the most ancient method of printing. The Egyptians used wood blocks to print their hieroglyphics, and the Chinese printed fabrics with wood blocks as early as the fourth century.

Etching is the second oldest method of printing. It dates back to the fifteenth century. The process of etching a design on metal is described on page 54.

PAINTS AND PRINTING

Before going into the steps for the various types of prints, let us consider the paints that can be used for printing and the specific prints to which they are best suited.

1. Tempera—poster paint or showcard colors—can be used on paper with stencils, block prints, and silk screen when a high degree of permanency is not required. Use water as a mixer and cleaner.

2. Oil colors are useful for block prints, stencils, and silk screen. When you use oil paints for block printing or stenciling, the secret is to mix as little turpentine with the colors as possible. Put in only enough to make the paints work well from your brush or roller. If too much is used, your design will run and look blurred on the edges. Turpentine is the mixer and cleaner.

3. Textile paints are for materials that are going to be washed or subjected to considerable wear. Use textile

colors and extender (a colorless pigment) and after the colors dry, place a dry cloth over the design and press the decorated areas with a hot iron. Plenty of heat sets textile colors best. Turn the material over and press on the back. After this, you may press again with a damp cloth. Textile paint or printing inks are recommended for all prints on fabrics. Extender is the mixer and cleaner.

4. Printing inks with a water or oil base are the best colors for block prints and are excellent when used for stencil or silk screen on paper and on fabric. The mixer and cleaner is water or turpentine depending on the type of ink you use.

MAKING PRINTS

Object and vegetable prints

Collect a variety of objects such as pieces of dowels, spools, erasers, corks, sponges, clothespins, shells, coiled pieces of corrugated paper. With these you can make interesting prints. You can cut simple notches in the dowels and spools and simple designs in the corks and erasers for more variety.

Potatoes and other vegetables such as turnips and carrots can create prints too. Cut them in half with one slice, so that the printing edge is smooth. It is well to have them cut a few hours before troop meeting and set face down on brown paper. They will be dry enough to work with. Cut a simple design in broad lines and masses. If the girls feel they need to draw a design first, they can transfer it by placing carbon paper between the vegetable and the design, and punching through into the vegetable with a pencil point.

Place a little paint (not too thin) on wax paper or a piece of glass, smooth it flat, and dip the object or vegetable in it. Print a few times on scrap paper until you see how much paint you need on the vegetable to make a smooth print. You may have to try quite a few prints because the vegetables should dry out enough, or may need more cutting. If your design fuzzes around the edges, your paint is too thin; if it smudges, the paint is too thick.

Try out your object and vegetable prints on a large sheet of paper. After you have tried a few, you can make a picture; a poster; a border design on a napkin, tablecloth,

24

or costume; an allover design for bookbinding paper or cloth, or wrapping paper; or a single motif for stationery.

Linoleum block prints

Linoleum is most practical for simple block printing. It is permanent, easily worked, and may be used to obtain a variety of effects.

You will need: plain colored linoleum (preferably battleship gray) or a linoleum block, paint or ink for printing, cleaner, paper or fabric on which to print, a piece of glass or tile, brayer, (also called a roller), newspapers, rags, stencil knife, sharp-pointed knife, or inexpensive set of linoleum cutting tools.

A simple design is usually the most effective. Plan it on paper and then transfer it to your linoleum by blackening the back of the design with a pencil or by using carbon paper and tracing the design. If there is lettering, remember to cut it into the block in reverse so that it prints correctly.

A stencil knife or any small sharp-pointed knife may be used for cutting. However, regular linoleum cutting tools —special V- or U-shaped gouges and sets consisting of 5 or 6 removable blades—are inexpensive and safest to use.

If the linoleum is old or cold, heat it for a few minutes in the sun or over a radiator or flame before you cut it. This makes the cutting easier and will enable you to get a smoother, more regular edge.

Outline the edges of the design with a V-shaped gouge or a stencil knife or razor blade, making a V-shaped cut (see illustration). If you stop with only the outline, it is called a white-line block, the printed design appearing in lines only. The second cutting technique is routing or digging out the areas not to be printed. Finally, there is the detailing, using the tools in a variety of ways to obtain interesting results and point up the details. Examine the work of some of the famous contemporary block printers.

Narrow spaces should be shallow, wide spaces should be deeper; in turning a corner or making a curve, turn the block rather than the tool. Check the outside edges before starting to print. A rough edge on a block or piece of linoleum can spoil the effect of an otherwise lovely print.

Spread the paint or printing ink from the tube onto the glass or tile and work the brayer over it. Roll the brayer back and forth until the "snap" is out of the ink and it is thoroughly inked. Roll the brayer over the cut block until there is an even coating of color. Place the block face down on the fabric or paper, and pound all over with a wooden mallet or step on it with your full weight evenly distributed, rocking back and forth. If you put several layers of newspaper or magazines under the surface on which you are printing, you will get a clearer print. Almost any kind of paper, even paper toweling, will take a block print, although one with a fairly dull surface and smooth grain is best. The professional block-printing paper is called rice paper. It is more expensive than ordinary paper, so use it for something special.

Clean your block with water or turpentine depending on the ink or paint used. Be especially careful to clean the ink out of the cuts of the linoleum design.

With a linoleum block print you can make a design for framing or for a wall hanging, greeting cards, bookplates, book covers and endpapers, tablecloths, place mats, aprons, smocks, and a variety of other items.

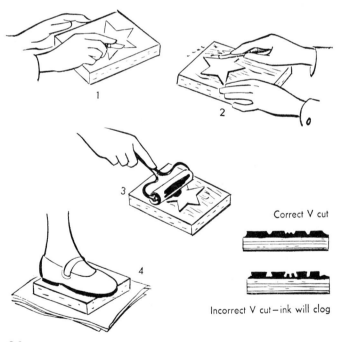

Correct V cut

Incorrect V cut—ink will clog

Stenciling

Stenciling is also an old art and can be used most effectively for a variety of purposes. It permits a wide range of colors and the covering of a larger area with colors, and the materials are usually less expensive than those for block printing. Stenciling can be used any place that a block print is suitable and, in addition, on wooden and metal objects, such as furniture, boxes, trays, walls. Early American designs on wallpaper, boxes, and chairs are good examples of the stencil technique.

You will need: stencil paper (purchased as such) or heavy wrapping paper or hard-finished cardboard; stencil brushes; stencil knife; razor blade, or small pointed scissors; paper or fabric on which to print; newspapers and rags; paint and its cleaner. See pages 23-24.

Plan your design in terms of how you intend to use it. Vegetables may be appropriate for a kitchen wall, but you wouldn't necessarily want them all over the pillows in the bedroom. Start by sketching or just freehand cutting a single, simple motif. Place it different ways and use different colors until you have arrived at a satisfactory allover pattern. If it is more than a really simple motif, draw the design on the stencil paper and then cut accurately around the drawn lines. It is essential that the cut lines be sharp and clean, leaving no ragged edges, for the holes are to be the painted part of the design. If your design begins to get more complicated, remember that all parts of the stencil must stay together, so be sure to leave connecting channels between parts of the design.

Tack the fabric or paper on which you are printing to a board or worktable. Make sure it is perfectly smooth. Pin or tack the stencil where you want it on the printing

Stenciling a three-color design

surface. Each color of your design requires a separate stencil and must be perfectly lined up. A large desk blotter under your work helps keep it neat and even.

Mix your ink or paints on a tile, plate, or glass to the color you desire. Dab the brush in the color without getting much ink on the brush—test on a piece of scrap paper. Apply the color to the fabric using short firm brush strokes, always working away from the edges of the stencil toward the center. Carefully remove the stencil when the area has been covered and your design will be complete.

If you wish to use shading, apply the color as above, then touch in a deeper shade. Two or more colors may be used; if the colors come close together, place a piece of blotting paper over the first part covered. If one color is to be used over another, always do the lighter color first, then the darker over it.

Materials best suited for stencil work are linen, cotton, and muslin.

There is no limit to the uses for the stenciling technique. It can be used on textiles, for curtains, articles of clothing, tablecloths and place mats, purses, beach bags or cushions; on the walls of a room; on furniture or other wooden articles. Your own needs and desires will add indefinitely to the list of uses.

Silk screening

Essentially this process is the stencil technique with a few variations. A fabric is stretched on a frame, a design is planned and is placed on the fabric by blocking out the background as described below. Paint is pressed through the open parts of the screen with a squeegee and thus the design is printed. Although silk screening is slightly more difficult and more expensive than stenciling, it has definite advantages. It is particularly suitable for designs that have to be turned out in quantity and in a hurry, such as programs for a fashion show or posters for a dance. It is used when a good clear print is desired. There is less chance of error in the printing process.

You will need: a frame, silk or organdy fabric about three inches larger than the frame, small tacks, tempera paint with which to print and its cleaner, squeegee, large blotter, paper on which to print, newspapers and rags.

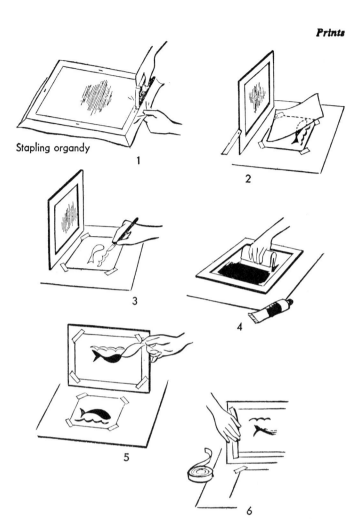

Stapling organdy

1

2

3

4

5

6

First you must make your screen. For this you will need cardboard, organdy, and a stapler.

Cut the outside dimensions of the cardboard 1½-2 inches larger than the print; the inside should be the same size as the print. Cut the organdy the size of the outside of the frame.

1. Staple the organdy to the cardboard frame, starting at the center of each side, pulling tight, and stapling the other sides.

Plan your design carefully in relation to the article on which you are going to use it and in relation to the size of the screen. Outline the design carefully.

2. Lay this design under thin pliable paper (not tissue) and fasten it carefully with tape.

29

3. Cut out the design with a sharp stencil knife, being sure not to cut into the original, just the thin paper.

4. Carefully adjust the original and the thin pattern on a printing board or flat surface so it will line up with the screen. Take off most of the tape, lower the screen, put some paint along one side, run squeegee across screen.

5. When you raise the screen, the thin paper will have separated from the original and adhered to the screen.

6. Now remove the original and reinforce the edges with strips of gummed paper. With a knife, strip out the cut area of the stencil. Now you are ready for printing.

To print your design, place your paper or fabric on the printing board and lower the screen. Be sure to place guide lines on this printing surface so that you can be sure the print is in the right place each time. Squeegee paint across the surface of the silk. Lift screen, remove paper; insert another sheet and squeegee paint across. Repeat until you have the number of prints you need. If you want to reprint the design later, save the original drawing and you can easily make another stencil and frame.

The cardboard screen is simple to make and is adequate for a few prints. However, it will not hold up as well as a wooden frame. For this you can use an old picture frame or you can make the frame.

The paper stencil method is quick and easy to do. The stencil can be removed and the screen used again if you use a wood frame. With this method, each color requires a separate stencil. More than one color is not practical for a cardboard frame.

There are other methods for preparing silk screen prints. Among these the film stencil method is fascinating and produces a clear-cut print. It is capable of making hundreds of prints with great detail. Other methods are the block-out method, tusche-resist method, and the photographic method. These produce prints more like original paintings and with less clearly defined outlines. You can learn about these methods from the books listed in the Bibliography.

bookbinding

There's real satisfaction in binding a book. It may be a treasure you've had for years that needs a new cover, or a book you have made yourself—illustrations, printing, and all. Many years ago, bookbinders were craftsmen important to the community because each book was a work of art. Recently, interest has been renewed in this art and artistic book covers are displayed at craftmen's shows.

This chapter describes just the most elementary steps in bookbinding that may be used to make a simple booklet, a portfolio, a book cover, or a scrapbook.

Think of the possibilities of combining bookbinding with the rest of the troop program. If the girls are working on badges related to trips or hiking, they could make their own scrapbook to keep a record of their trips. Or, if it's a badge related to learning more about their state or country, they could keep maps in a handmade portfolio. In addition, the other hand arts may be used in working on bookbinding. Any printing method, watercolor painting, or the marbleizing process described in the chapter on "Paper" may be used to decorate the portfolios. The girls may embroider fabric or do chip carving for the scrapbooks.

In any case, help the girls to use good taste by keeping the design in proportion to the size of the finished article. Small patterns are generally best, and an overabundance

31

of pattern may be avoided by keeping either the cover or the lining a solid color.

DESCRIPTION OF MATERIALS

HEAVY CARDBOARD about ⅛-¼ inch in thickness. Chip board is usually used. This can be purchased in art supply stores. Ask for it by the thickness desired. It is best cut with a sharp knife or single-edged blade.

VEGETABLE GLUE OR WHITE PASTE. The recipe for the rye flour in the chapter on "Leather" can also be used.

BINDER'S LINEN, which is a specially prepared material used for the spine of the book. It may be purchased at art supply stores or bookbinders. Or, use any firm but not bulky cotton or linen fabric such as denim, cotton twill, Indian Head. Lightweight leather can also be used.

LINING. The lining can be any smooth fabric that is not bulky or sleazy. Use one of those named above, or broadcloth, percale, chintz. The lining can also be a pliable, opaque, decorative paper.

DECORATIVE COVER. The decorative cover gives you a wide choice of materials. You may use any of the fabrics mentioned above plus burlap, thin leathers, and many types of decorative papers that are pliable—wallpaper, imported Italian or Japanese papers, marbleized papers, or some decorated by the girls. Needlepoint and embroidery may be used.

SHELLAC OR PLASTIC SPRAY for paper covers to give it a protective coat from soil and fingermarks.

In addition you will need scissors, hole punch, ruler, wax paper, and clean cloths.

THINGS TO MAKE

Simple booklet

This little booklet is simple but it is a good introduction to the art of bookbinding. A little book can have a variety of uses: for notes, telephone numbers, or addresses. You can also use the same method to make a much larger booklet.

You will need: several layers of unruled paper cut the same size (about 6 x 5 inches), thin cardboard or heavy paper 8 x 7 inches, needle and strong thread.

You can put the cover decoration directly on the heavy paper or cover the thin cardboard with paper or fabric.

Cut the paper or fabric 1 inch larger than cardboard on all sides, glue to cardboard, mitering corners.

Line the cover with the lightweight fabric (see "Lining") to within ⅛ inch of edges.

Fold the pages and the cover in the center. Open them and hold them flat. Punch a hole (with a large needle) through them in the center of the fold of the inner page.

Punch 2 corresponding holes above and below the center, equally spaced until 5 holes have been made. Start sewing at the inner center of the book, leaving sufficient thread to be tied later. Carry thread through the center hole out of the cover, in again through the next hole, and out the next. Sew in and out up to the top hole, down to the bottom and back to the center. When the thread returns to the center, loop it over the sewed portion and tie with a firm double knot. Keep the thread taut but do not pull tightly because the thread will cut the paper. Fold the book into position and put under a weight to dry.

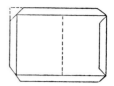
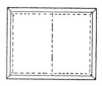
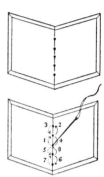

Simple booklet

Portfolio

You can make a portfolio of any size. Measure the pictures you want to protect with a portfolio and cut your pieces in the same proportion as those given below.

You can use either cloth or paper for the cover and for the lining, so we will refer to these as the covering and lining material, whichever it may be.

The pictures to go in this portfolio are 11 x 14 inches. The first procedure is to cut the following:

2 pieces of heavy cardboard, 12 x 15 inches

1 outside hinge cloth, 3½ x 16 inches

1 hinge cloth lining, 3½ x 15 inches

2 pieces of decorative material for cover, 12½ x 17 inches

2 lining pieces, 11 x 14¾ inches

6 tapes, 5 inches long.

These figures are, of course, just guides to help you with your first project. You can vary the dimensions, and make such changes as putting the cover or lining (if it's fabric) and hinge all in one. After you've made one, you will see how simple the process is and be able to make your own variations.

With all the pieces, your paste before you, the table covered, and a ruler nearby, you are ready to start.

Glue the hinge to the front and back covers so that the hinge extends 1 inch over each cardboard.

Glue the hinge lining in place, then glue down the extending ends of the hinge cloth. To place the tapes, mark a point on the inside covers 1 inch from the center of the top, bottom, and open side. Glue the tapes at this point, and glue a small piece of lightweight fabric over the tapes.

The cover material needs to be very smooth and straight. Make sure your hands are clean and that you have a clean cloth nearby. The cover material is cut so that it extends 1 inch beyond the top, bottom, and open end. The side coming to the hinge is turned under ¼ inch and extends ¼ inch over the hinge. (In order to get a smooth fold on paper, draw the fold line with a dull table knife on the wrong side of the paper.) Spread the paste smoothly over the outside of one cover board. Place the cover material in place, and carefully smooth with a clean cloth from the center to the edges to remove bumps and bubbles. Cover the other board in the same manner. When both are glued in place, glue down the extending inch, mitering the corners. Smooth these sections also, this time from the outside in.

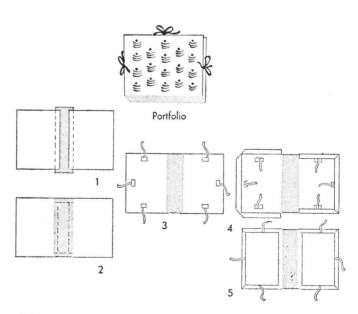

Portfolio

The lining is glued in place so that it comes to about ⅛ inch from 3 sides and just slightly laps over the hinge lining cloth. Again smooth after glueing in place.

Cover the inside covers with wax paper and place under a weight to dry. Place the fabric hinge inside the covers before putting under the weight. This will give it an even crease. It should dry a day or two for best results. Whenever you use fabric, be sure it is cut and pasted with the weave going straight up and down. Placed on the diagonal, it will pucker.

Book cover

This book cover is made on exactly the same principles as the other bindings. It is an excellent cover for a book that you want to protect or for one that you want to make better looking—perhaps a telephone book.

Measure the book for which you are making a cover. Take exact measurements of the cover and the depth of the book. Let us assume that the book you are covering measures 5½ x 8¼ inches and is ¾ of an inch thick. You would, therefore, cut the following materials:

2 coverboards, 6 x 9 inches
1 cardboard for back (spine), 9 x 1 inches
1 thin cardboard, 8½ x ¾ inches
1 piece hinge cloth, 11 x 3½ inches
1 piece hinge cloth lining, 9 x 3 inches
1 back cardboard lining, 9½ x 1½ inches

Book cover

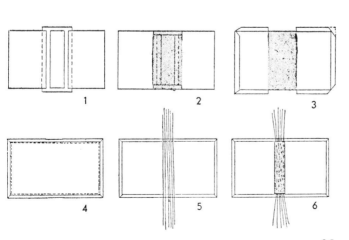

35

2 pieces cover material, 6½ x 11 inches
2 pieces cover lining, 5 x 9 inches
5 cords, 2 times length of book plus enough to knot.

Assemble the book cover in the following steps:

1. Glue two cover cardboards and one back cardboard on the hinge cloth so that hinge cloth extends 1 inch over each cover board and there is ¼ inch between covers and back board. Turn down, and glue extending ends of hinge cloth.

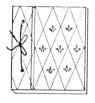

Scrapbook

2. Glue the lining of the hinge in place.

3. Glue cover material in place. Turn cover material under ¼ inch on length, bringing folded edge ¼ inch over hinge, miter corners, fold over and glue.

4. Glue lining of covers in place to within ⅛ inch of edges of three sides.

5. Cover thin cardboard with lining material.

6. Glue cords in place on back cardboard.

7. Cover the cords with the thin cardboard piece, wrong side glued against cords.

8. Place wax paper over entire piece, put weight in center, and let dry for one or two days.

9. Insert book in cover and tie on with the cords.

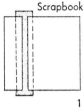

1

2

Scrapbook

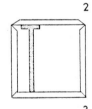

3

Is there anyone who doesn't collect something? Some people like poems, leaves, clippings, or pictures, but practically everyone can use a good-looking scrapbook.

Making a scrapbook can be an excellent project for camp, or for when a troop is preparing for a trip. You can keep in your handmade scrapbook mementoes of all the wonderful adventures you had. Somehow it makes the whole experience just that much more exciting.

Let us assume for this project we have pages 10 x 14 inches. Cut the following pieces:

1 piece heavy cardboard, 10½ x 14½ inches
1 piece heavy cardboard, 1½ by 14½ inches
1 piece heavy cardboard, 8¾ x 14½ inches
1 piece binder's linen, 2¼ x 15½ inches
2 pieces cover material, 12½ x 16½ inches
2 pieces lining cloth, 10½ x 14½ inches
1 cord, 2 times the length plus enough to knot.

4

Assemble these pieces in the following steps:

1. Glue the cardboards 8¾ x 14½ and 1½ x 14½ to the hinge fabric leaving a ¼-inch space between boards.

2. Turn down extensions and glue.

3. Cover front and back cardboards as for book cover.

4. Line covers as for book cover.

5. Punch holes in back cardboard and narrow part of front cardboard to correspond.

6. Cover with wax paper and place under weight to dry.

7. Place paper in position and lace with cord.

The shellac or plastic spray can be used on a paper cover material for added protection.

This type of scrapbook can be made with wood. Instead of making the hinge from binder's linen use small metal hinges from a hardware store or make leather hinges and screw on with tiny screws. Drill holes and lace with leather thonging. This scrapbook is especially adaptable to camping situations. You can decorate the cover by chip carving, wood burning, gesso, or any other method described in the chapter on "Wood."

wood

Woodworking is a very versatile hand art and one for which the material is generally easy to obtain. It offers a challenge to creative ability, and there is a real sense of satisfaction to be gained from the finished project. There is adventure, too, in just finding the right kind of wood.

Many different kinds of wood can be used. The familiar pieces of "sidewalk lumber" are readily available—orange crates, cigar boxes, packing cases, berry boxes, and scraps from the lumberyard. This wood is already seasoned as is wood that has been lying on the ground for some time. Other wood should be dried or seasoned or it will split later. Woods range from soft to very hard. The beginner should start with a softwood—balsa wood or pine, bass, poplar, white wood, red gum. Later she can work with woods of medium hardness—mahogany, black walnut, and finally the hardwoods—cherry, birch, oak, and hard maple. The softwoods cut more easily but are not as durable.

Working in wood can be combined with the other fields of interest. For example, the study of trees in nature, furniture design in homemaking, making equipment in sports and games and the out-of-doors. The girls can find examples of the woodworkers' art in their own homes, in churches and museums.

38

CARVING

Producing or decorating by cutting figures and designs is the art of wood carving. It's a fine activity for a Girl Scout troop. The first step is learning to use a knife, which, besides the wood, is the only material needed. The *Junior Girl Scout Handbook* gives instructions for using a jackknife.

There are many ways to start. One is to use a piece of dried wood to make a doll. Many countries have such simple and charming wooden dolls as those shown. In Japan, they are called Koeshi dolls, meaning dolls carved from a tree. They are a wonderful beginning project or an advanced project, for that matter. The lines are nice, simple, and uncomplicated. After you arrive at the desired shape, sand and paint it in a colorful design with enamel or oil paints (see page 43). Other such small, simple articles for the beginner are found in the illustration below. Perhaps you may want to try carving animals. Whatever your choice, keep the outline simple and don't try to make a "real-looking" animal. The little Swedish horse gives you an idea of the simplicity to strive for in a "first" project. It is very effective when painted with gay designs.

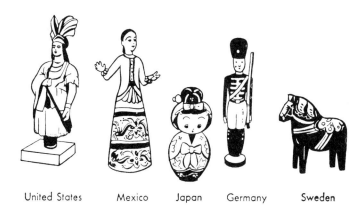

United States   Mexico   Japan   Germany   Sweden

After the preliminary steps of whittling a small object, your next design can be blocked out. Saw away the wood outside the lines of the design (see page 42). Finish the object with your knife. Some objects may be left with the knife marks showing; others need to be sanded down, perhaps stained, and finally polished with wax.

39

A good way to start learning to carve heads and faces is to use old spools from the sewing basket. The wood carves easily and you can make a variety of heads or other figures. If someone you know plays chess, why not start a chess set? There are other games for which figures may be made. Making games and toys for hospitals and orphanages is a really creative service project.

You can use scraps of wood for objects of wearing apparel, for use in the home, as well as for figures and animals for decoration. With the help of a saw, you can make interesting wooden buckles, pins, or buttons with just a few notches for a design.

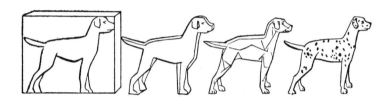

For pins or buttons, notch a little groove in the back and fill in with plastic wood which comes in tubes at hardware stores. Insert a pin back or a small metal loop for buttons. To make the fork-and-spoon salad set pictured below, use the same principles of blocking out, cutting away the unused portions of the design, and finishing the details with your knife. Sand your pieces well and give them a good polish. You may rub in linseed oil to darken a little and finish by rubbing with a coat of paste wax.

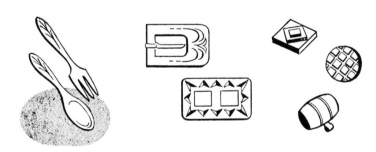

CONSTRUCTION PROCESSES

There are many items that you can construct, but we have described only a few. For more advanced processes and more ideas, look for books in your local library. Although many tools may be used in constructing articles of wood, the illustration shows only a few inexpensive ones that a troop or camp could easily buy or borrow.

USING A SAW. Whatever you wish to cut out, the principle of using the coping saw is the same. See illustration on page 42 for position. Hold it lightly in your hand and do not apply too much pressure.

The coping saw is useful for any small project you may wish to do, but it is too light for thick pieces and larger construction work. You can use heavier or lighter blades depending upon the thickness of the wood. Always place the teeth of the blade downward.

Woodworking tools

keyhole saw

hand drill and bit   file

C-clamp

plane

coping saw   screwdriver   try-square

claw hammer

USING A V BLOCK enables you to get into the corners and produce finer detail. However, do not design an object

41

that has too many protruding parts. If you do not have a vise, you can clamp the V block to the edge of the table with a small clamp.

Let your first project be simple, such as a pair of book ends. To increase your skill in sawing, try something a little more complicated with a piece of plywood or other thin wood. You can make effective decorations for a Christmas tree, a mobile, a space sculpture decoration for a wall, a plaque to hold keys, or mats for hot dishes. Sometimes you will not be able to keep sawing around the outline of your figure. In such cases, saw from the edge of the wood into the outline in several places. For corners, turn the wood rather than the saw.

When your piece is completely sawed out, smooth the edges with fine sandpaper and finish by painting a design or applying one of the finishes described on page 45.

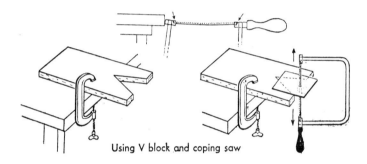

Using V block and coping saw

THINGS TO MAKE

Book ends

For this project, you can use the ends of orange crates. Work on a pattern until one satisfies you, then transfer it lightly onto the wood by blackening the back of the paper with a pencil and drawing over the design. Then saw along the line you have made. To complete your book ends, use a thinner piece of wood for the base and nail it to the side piece with small nails. Sand the book ends until they are smooth to the touch. Apply any of the decorations described later in this chapter and finish. You can apply a design of your own in metal foil, leather, or fabric, if you wish. See the chapters on these subjects to give you more ideas.

A frame

Perhaps you have a favorite print or a painting that you would like to frame. To make a simple frame, you need the following supplies: a piece of plywood the size of your print, four pieces of lattice strips, two cut to the size of the plywood and two cut to fit flush without mitering, small wire nails, water-soluble glue, shellac or plastic spray. Glue your print to the plywood back. Decorate the lattice strips, if you wish, with gold paper, copper foil, leather, paint, or apply a finish. Then when this is dry, nail these to the plywood as shown. Cover your picture with clear plastic spray or clear shellac. Rub the back of the plywood lightly with fine steel wool and put on a coat of paint or shellac and a final coat of paste wax.

DECORATING WOOD

Painting

A design can be painted on the natural wood or on wood that has been given a background color. However, if the grain does not show up well, or the wood has been discolored, give the wood two or three coats of enamel. If you are using new wood, you also need one base coat of sealer.

Use a basic color for your background so that the design will show up well. When you use the natural wood, give the piece a coat of clear shellac before painting on a design. This seals the pores of the wood and prevents the colors from running. Whether your background is enamel paint or shellac, when it is dry rub lightly with fine steel wool. You may use a planned design or a freehand drawing. If you do plan your design on paper first, trace it lightly on the wood. Use oil colors or enamels for painting the design. When the colors have dried thoroughly, finish the piece with shellac or varnish.

For an antique finish on light-colored painted backgrounds or natural wood color, mix burnt umber oil paint with turpentine to a thin mixture and rub it lightly over the entire object. With a clean cloth wipe the excess off the main portions, leaving it darker in corners.

You can make a beautiful object this way by applying a design to a small wooden bowl, wooden boards to use for cheeseboards, cigar boxes for a variety of uses, wooden shaving soap bowls, round wooden cheeseboxes, or just a square of scrapwood for a hot dish mat.

Gesso

Another method of applying a decoration to wood is the ancient Egyptian art of gesso. Gesso is a white, creamlike mixture when mixed to the proper consistency. You can buy it in powder form in art supply or hardware stores (directions for mixing are on the can), or you can make it yourself from the following directions:

Mix 16 tablespoons whiting with water to thick cream consistency. Stir in 12 tablespoons liquid glue, 2 tablespoons varnish, and 8 of linseed oil, mix thoroughly. Boil in double boiler for ten minutes. This makes about 1 pint of mixture.

Whiting can be purchased in dry form in hardware stores.

Sketch your design lightly on the wood. Fill in the design with brushloads of gesso. The result will be a raised design. You can add color to the gesso itself by adding tempera, or you can use oil color to paint over the raised design after it is completed. Then give your article a finish such as described on page 45.

Chip carving

Chip carving is a decoration given to wood by carving or chipping out a design with two or more sharp knives called a sticking-out knife and a slicing knife. A variety of designs are possible but they are usually geometric and constructed with ruler, pencil, and compass beforehand to assure absolutely accurate lines.

Chip carving may be worked on the top of a softwood box, on a piece of scrap wood to be used as a hot dish mat, or a larger flat piece to be used as a scrapbook cover. You can decorate a frame or make a paperweight from a square piece of wood.

You will need: softwood article, small pieces of wood on which to experiment, chip-carving knives or a sharp, single-edged razor blade, sandpaper, and finish.

Work out your design on paper and trace it on the wood. First outline the triangle you wish to chip out by making sharp precise lines with the sticking knife held straight up. With the point of the blade at center of triangle, make three straight cuts out to the points of the triangle. The chipping is done with the slicing knife held at an angle and pressing toward the center lines. You may also use a single-edged razor blade for both these operations. Experiment on a scrap of softwood with any of the tools until you get the "feel." To finish your work, sand it lightly with fine sandpaper (Grade 00000), then to highlight the carving you may darken it by brushing on an oil-penetrating stain and wiping it off quickly, or rubbing on some burnt umber oil paint thinned with turpentine. When it's dry, use one of the finishes.

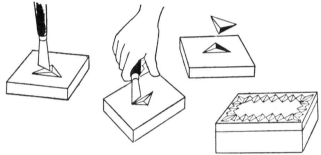

FINISHES

Before finishing, the wood should be smooth and clean. It should be sanded several times with increasingly fine sandpaper and then steel wool, also increasingly fine. To put a stain on wood before a finish, use an oil-penetrating stain. It can be bought in shades of mahogany, maple, or pine and can be mixed to achieve the color you desire.

Linseed oil and wax

Although you may have an article that you want just waxed, we will not consider that one of the actual finishes but will start with linseed oil and wax. This finish sounds easy to do, but it takes months to do well. It also darkens the wood.

You will need: linseed oil (boiled) and paste wax, several cloths, pumice or rottenstone.

Rub a little linseed oil into the wood with the palm of your hand, about one coat a month for six months. When you finally achieve the luster and smoothness you desire, polish with pumice or rottenstone on a soft cloth. Protect

45

the entire finish with a coat of paste wax and rub it down smooth.

Shellac and wax

You will need: shellac thinned with alcohol, paste wax, soft cloths, cheesecloth to apply the shellac. Shellac comes in two colors, clear and orange. The clear is the basic shellac, the orange is used to tint the clear, especially for an antique effect.

Apply three or four coats of shellac, thinning each coat with three or more parts of wood alcohol to each part shellac. It is too hard to handle the shellac much thicker. Pour some into a jar or can and soak up a little on a cheesecloth folded into a round pad. Apply your shellac evenly over the entire piece. Let that coat dry thoroughly. On warm days in the direct sun, it may take three hours, but ordinarily it is best to let each coat dry overnight. Humid days are not good for shellacking because the alcohol attracts moisture from the air and gives a white film to the coat of shellac. When this happens, there is nothing to do but remove the whitened coat with alcohol and start again another day.

After each coat dries, rub down the piece with very fine grade steel wool. Use Grade 000 for rubbing the undercoat and Grade 0000 or finer for the final coat. After the last rubbing down, a coat of paste wax is given to the piece and it is rubbed softly to polish. Clean your cloths with alcohol, which is the solvent for shellac.

Varnish

For a piece that needs a hard finish, resistant to heat, water and alcohol, varnish is the answer. A good sanding job before you start to apply the finish will give you a smooth, final job.

You will need: varnish, wax, steel wool, several soft cloths.

Brush on or apply with cheesecloth one of the quick-drying, synthetic varnishes, and let it dry thoroughly. A second coat of varnish will finish the job. Rub lightly with very fine steel wool and put on a final coat of paste wax.

You can remove old paint or varnish with paint or varnish remover and an old table knife or scraper. After removing the finish, sand well before applying a new finish.

metal

Working with metal is an art in which the girls can really let themselves go. They can pound and bend and make a lot of noise, but be sure they are in a room where the noise won't disturb the janitor or the lady upstairs. But some metalwork requires delicate, fine work. Metal is sturdy and durable, and your girls can make some very useful objects.

In the early days of our country, the settlers turned out beautiful and simple metalwork to meet their everyday needs. For example, they made candle sconces, kitchen utensils, weather vanes, tin boxes, trays, and lanterns. Later on, they started using silver, and today we can still find the influence of the famous silversmith, Paul Revere.

Metalwork can be very simple, even if you've never tried it before. The most adaptable metals for use in Girl Scout troops and camps are tin, pewter, copper, and brass. They can be soldered and they can be used alone or in combination to make very effective pieces of art. However, the kind of metal you choose depends on how much you wish to spend, how difficult it is to work with, and what the object you make is to be used for.

Wire and foil are easy to work with, and, therefore, are suitable for the youngest Brownie. Heavier metal is sometimes hard to cut or bend, so younger girls may not have

47

enough strength. Metals are classified by gauge number and 16 gauge is satisfactory for bowls, plates, and most metalwork. Lighter weights are higher numbers and heavier weights are lower numbers. Soldering and etching are activities that probably should be reserved for Cadette and Senior Scouts because of the more technical steps involved.

METAL FOIL

One type of metal for which you need no previous experience is copper or brass foil, yet both the beginner and the professional find it most satisfying. A tooled or punched design in foil or copper paper may be used to add a decorative touch to wooden boxes, book ends, bookcases, or furniture. The foil may also be designed to use as Christmas decorations, such as those made in the Scandinavian countries, or as a centerpiece or mobile.

Foil is a lightweight piece of metal about 32 gauge and usually comes in a roll. You can purchase it by the foot in art supply or hardware stores. Copper building paper, although not really foil, offers unlimited possibilities. It can be cut with scissors, punched, tooled, and joined to a backing with copper tacks, rivets, or linoleum cement.

Tooled designs

Tooling foil is done with a small blunt stick, such as an orange stick, with a pad of newspapers under the work. After the foil is cut to size, the design is pressed into the foil with the stick. It is pressed on the right side for indented lines or masses and on the wrong side for raised masses. The raised portions are filled in from the back with plastic wood, sawdust and glue, or cotton and glue.

As a last step the background is smoothed flat on a hard surface, with the flat end of the orange stick.

Punched designs

Designs may be punched with a small, sharp, pointed nail, awl, or ice pick, using an old board for backing. Plan your design carefully. You can draw it on the foil with a pencil or tape the paper in position over the foil. Now punch the design into the foil.

Finishing

To finish, rub the foil lightly with fine emery cloth. If the foil has darkened, go over it with a soft cloth dipped in vinegar and salt or copper polish. Rub to develop a sheen and to preserve the luster. Put on a coat of wax, shellac, or clear plastic spray.

If you want a darkened effect on copper, dip the foil design in a solution of liver of sulphur (potassium sulphide, 1½-inch cube crushed in 1½ cups of water). Let it turn black, remove it from the solution and wash well. Polish the highlights with fine steel wool, an emery cloth, or fine wet pumice. Polish again with a soft dry cloth.

WIRE

Wire is an excellent medium for developing creative expression as well as for producing something beautiful and useful. It is inexpensive, easy to store, and available at all hardware stores. There are wires of alloys, copper, and silver. Although easily bent, wire will hold its shape, and can be taken apart and used again.

With wire you can make faces or plaques, three-dimensional sculpture figures, mobiles, and jewelry. Use your imagination and experiment with various combinations. The only materials you need are wire, a wire cutter or tin snips, and a pair of small pliers. Other items or tools may be added after the girls decide upon a project.

Wire sculpture

THREE-DIMENSIONAL SCULPTURE. For this type of sculpture, bend the wire (14 gauge or less or coat hangers) with pliers following a sketch or just freehand. Your sculp-

ture should stand evenly on a flat surface. You can achieve this by bending the metal into a base or mounting your finished work on a wooden base. There aren't any rules for this type of sculpture—bend the wire until it pleases you. Your design may represent animals or people or just nothing at all. For the first try, encourage the girls to design something that doesn't have to be soldered. Have the girls bring in items such as beads, button molds, pieces of screen or colored glass, scraps of metal. All these can be used effectively in sculpture or in hanging sculptures, which are called "mobiles" (see page 9).

FLAT WIRE SCULPTURES can be produced from a sketch with 14- 16-gauge wire, pliers and perhaps a mallet to flatten the design. A better method, however, is to use a piece of plywood or scrap lumber and nails as a pattern or jig. Sketch the design first, and when this is satisfactory, transfer it to the wood. Place a nail at intervals where there is a curve in the design. Straighten the wire until there are no kinks or bumps. Then start with one end of wire and form it around the nails into your design. When you have finished, lift the design from the wood. You can add such items as screen, paper, and glass mentioned for three-dimensional sculpture.

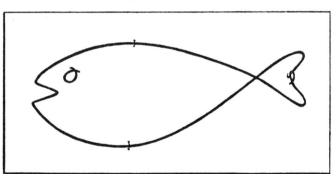

Wire jewelry

Copper and silver wire jewelry pieces are easy to make and very handsome. Practice first with less expensive alloy wire. Use 16- or 18-gauge wire or a higher gauge for finer work. The design shown in the illustration is adapted from bronze jewelry made over three thousand years ago. The links are coiled with pliers and placed together without any soldering.

More elaborate patterns can be made on a board with nails to guide the pattern. This is called a jig and you can use it to make bracelets, pins, necklaces. Make your own pattern by the placement of the nails. Some designs may be linked together with small rings bent around a nail or a roundnose pliers.

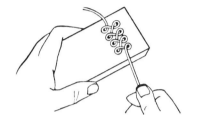 

TIN

The first thing that comes to mind when mentioning tin is that old standby, the tin can. It is inexpensive and has a variety of uses. The *Junior Girl Scout Handbook* and other books on camping give suggestions for making camp equipment from tin cans.

Think of the articles you have seen that are made in the shape of a tin can. Some examples are a watering can, small pitcher, plant holder, lantern, and letter basket. The tin in a can is lightweight and, therefore, is not usable for plates, bowls, or letter openers. There are many other things that can be made by cutting part of the tin can away, or by cutting it completely apart and using the flattened tin. Such articles include thermometer holders, candle sconces, planters, figures, and picture frames. For all, except the last suggestion, sheet tin gives a sturdier and longer lasting product. You can purchase sheet tin at a tinsmith's shop.

The basic materials you need are: ruler, tin snips, work gloves, wooden or plastic head mallet, wooden block, small pliers, tin, and, sometimes, solder.

Always finish the edges of the articles so they will not cut. Wear gloves while working. If you put a handle or design on the article, do it in permanent form—join the piece by soldering and apply the design with permanent paint so the tin won't rust.

51

Decorating tin

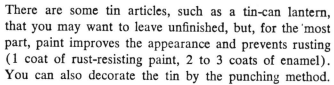

There are some tin articles, such as a tin-can lantern, that you may want to leave unfinished, but, for the 'most part, paint improves the appearance and prevents rusting (1 coat of rust-resisting paint, 2 to 3 coats of enamel). You can also decorate the tin by the punching method.

PAINTING. First, give your object a coat of metal primer, then 2 or 3 coats of gloss enamel or flat enamel. Black is a good background color. Let this dry. Plan your design and apply it to the can. The best method is free-hand. Just strokes with a small paint brush make a very effective design. Keep the line simple and don't overdecorate. Your decoration can be applied in oil colors or enamels.

PUNCHING. The usual method of decorating tin-can articles, other than painting, is punching. Such designs were used in tin work in the early colonies. To make a punched design, place a log inside the tin can. The wood should be nearly as large as the tin can. Then, with a hammer and nail, punch your design on the tin after carefully laying it out in pencil. Or tape a paper pattern to the tin and punch through both the pattern and the tin.

Watering can

To make a watering can, you need one tin can for the body and one can from which to cut the handle. If you want a long spout, you will also need a piece of copper tubing (purchase from hardware store or plumber), a hand drill with a bit the size of the tubing, and solder.

First clean the can and smooth the surface with steel wool. To make a small spout, place the pliers as shown and twist to the right, then place it on the other side and twist to the left. For the long spout, drill a hole in the can where you want to attach the spout. Insert copper tubing and solder in place.

Make a paper pattern for the handle to determine how long you need it to enable you to get your fingers between the handle and the can. Cut the other can and flatten. Trace the pattern on flat tin and cut out the handle. Fold the edges as described on page 57. Shape the handle with the pliers, and solder it to the can.

If there are any sharp edges, file them smooth. Now

give the finished article a coat of rust-resisting primer, 2 or 3 coats of black paint, and decorate it with your own design.

Flour scoop

For this item, draw the outline on the tin and cut away the rest of the can with tin snips. File the edges because you cannot make a folded edge on the curve. With hand drill and bit, drill a hole in the bottom of the can. Use a small round drawer pull for the handle. Put screw through hole and fasten with a nut (see illustration).

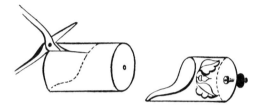

COPPER

Needless to say, all the items mentioned under "Tin" can be made in copper. All the same techniques can be used. However, copper is usually too expensive for the beginner, so we suggest you make the few items in tin first to get the feel of working in metal, and then progress to copper. For the most part, articles made in copper should not be painted since the beauty of the metal itself is better than any painted decoration that could be put on. We have chosen as our examples small articles that can be made by girls in troops and camps. For both of these you will need the sandbag and covered mallet described below.

SANDBAG. To make this simple sandbag which will enable you to work anywhere, you need a piece of sturdy pillow ticking or other closewoven fabric about 18 x 36 inches, and enough sand to fill the bag. Fold in half to make a square 18 x 18 inches. Sew up 2¾ sides of the bag on a machine. Pour in the sand and finish sewing by hand. It is very important to get the bag packed full and very tight with the sand.

COVERED MALLET. If you do not have a plastic head mallet and are using a wooden mallet, you will discover that it leaves small indented marks. If you would rather have the copper smooth, you can cover the mallet with felt or leather. Draw a circle on the leather or felt about an inch larger than the head of the mallet and tack it on to the side you are using.

Bowl

You will need: a disk of copper, covered wooden or plastic head mallet, sandbag.

The copper disk is placed on the sandbag and it is shaped by a steady rhythmical beat of the mallet on the copper. Revolve the disk as you pound. Work the blows of the mallet from the outside down to the center of the bowl until it is as deep as you wish it to be. If you have access to an oven, a kiln, or bonfire, it makes for easier shaping if you heat the metal slightly before working on it. Refer to section on "Metal Foil" for polishing and oxidizing the copper.

Etched pin

Etching copper is a fascinating medium that can produce handsome objects with a minimum of material. It is better to work out-of-doors because of the fumes of the acid. You can use this method effectively on paper knives, buckles, napkin rings or clips, bracelets, and many other items. We merely use a pin as an example.

You will need: a small disk of copper, mallet, sandbag, asphaltum, diluted nitric acid (3 parts water to 1 part acid), a pin back, a small wide-mounted glass dish such as a Pyrex custard cup, work gloves, kerosene or turpentine, soft cloths, small paint brush, large pan of water.

First, dome your disk slightly. This gives it a more interesting shape than a flat circle. The doming is accomplished in the same way as making the bowl on page 54. Place your design on the convex side of the copper with carbon paper, going over the lines afterward with a pencil to give it a clear outline. Your designs, at first, should not be fine or intricate because the etching process is more adaptable to simple, bold designs. Whatever you do *not* want to be etched, paint with black asphaltum. This should be applied smoothly and evenly to prevent any acid from getting through to the copper. You may have the design etched or the background etched. Don't forget to cover the entire back and the edges of your pin with the asphaltum too!

Pour the acid from its container to the small Pyrex dish. Pour enough to cover your metal pin. It is much safer if you buy the acid from the druggist already mixed with the water instead of trying to mix it yourself. If you do have to mix it yourself, *be sure to ask the pharmacist how to do it*. Leave the article in the acid bath until the metal is eaten away to the desired depth. An easy way to remove the disk from the acid is to pour the acid back in its container, with your work gloves on of course, without trying to get the disk out. Then rinse the dish with clear water several times and when all traces of the acid are removed, remove your copper pin from the glass. Be extremely careful not to touch anything that has come in contact with acid until it has been thoroughly rinsed. Although some articles are not small enough for the custard cup, be sure to put the acid in a *glass* container only. The only substitute for a glass container you may use is black roofing paper folded up at the corners to make a tray of the desired size.

The next process is removing the asphaltum with kerosene or turpentine. This will take a little rubbing. You may wish to leave some of the asphaltum on the piece. Very interesting effects can be obtained with a combination of the black and copper color. When you have finished, wash your pieces carefully in soap and water. Polish with a soft cloth. You may need to brush slightly with an emery cloth any spots on the edge or portion where the acid came through and made a pockmark. The edges should be smooth and beveled.

Apply the pin back with cold solder or with the regular soldering technique. Make sure your pin is facing the correct way for you to fasten it easily. If you wish to darken the copper, refer to the finishing technique on page 49.

Other metals can also be etched but they require a different acid solution. Refer to books listed in the Bibliography.

METAL PROCESSES

Cutting

Metal foil can be cut with ordinary scissors. Lightweight metals such as tin and "do-it-yourself" aluminum can be cut with heavy shears or tin snips. The girls should wear work gloves when they are cutting tin with shears because the edges are quite sharp. A good pair of tin snips will cut straight lines or curves smoothly and easily.

Sawing

Heavier metals (copper, silver) have to be sawed with a jeweler's or coping saw. There are times when you must saw the lighter metals, for example, to make a pin that has a cut-out section.

For sawing an outline of an article, in addition to the saw, you need a V block, clamp, and jeweler's file. Draw the design on the surface of the metal so that the lines show plainly. Clamp the V block to the table as shown on page 42. Hold the metal on the V block with one hand. The saw blade is always placed in the saw with teeth pointing down. Place the teeth on the edge of the metal on the line to be sawed and move the saw up and down easily without much pressure. The looser you hold your saw the better it will be. You are less likely to break the blade in this way.

For a cut-out section, you will also need a hand drill with a bit larger than the blade of the coping saw. In the middle of the section you want removed, drill a hole. Remove the top end of the saw blade from the frame, push it up through the hole in the metal and replace it in the frame. Start the sawing action again, holding the saw very

56

loosely. Work out to the outlines and around it until the section falls out. Move the metal on the V block rather than the saw.

Bending

Some metals are easier to bend than others—the lighter the gauge, the easier it is bent. Bending is necessary in edge finishing. To bend metal, use a block of wood with a sharp straight edge. For a straight bend, first draw a line with a ruler exactly where the bend should be, then place the edge of the wood almost to the line and bend the piece over the wood. The edges may need a tap with the mallet. You can also use a worktable edge if it is not too rounded. The process is essentially the same for any bend. For a rounded bend, you also need pliers. Hold part of the metal with left hand, with pliers in right hand bring the bend around toward you. To make a circle, you may need to bend the metal around a circular object, table leg, etc.

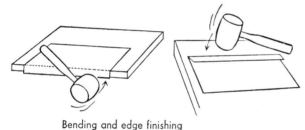

Bending and edge finishing

Edge finishing

All edges in metal should be finished so that they are smooth and will not cut. This may be done in two ways. On lightweight metal you can fold edges over. It is necessary that anything like a handle that is going to be used should be smooth to the touch.

FOLDED EDGE. Draw a pencil line with a ruler about ⅛ inch from the edge to be folded. Place this fold on your wooden block and, with the mallet, make downward strokes on the edge until the metal is folded over 45 degrees. Then place the metal right side down and with strokes of the mallet toward the inside, bend the metal edge over until it is flat against itself. Pound the entire edge flat. This makes a nice firm edge. If you hold it

57

firmly while folding and pounding, it makes a very straight edge.

FILING. Edges that are not folded should be filed with a jeweler's file. These are small files. You can also use finely cut wood files for some work. The jeweler's file is handy because it can get in small places. It can be purchased round, triangular, flat, half round, and square. You need to file the rounded edges of items like the sconce, scoop, the inside of the cut-out project, any piece of jewelry, and any edge on heavier metal. Folding over is only practical for lightweight metals.

Joining

SOFT SOLDERING is useful for tin, and some copper pieces. It is not useful for a piece that has a great deal of soldering to be done. If the sections to be soldered are close together, the heat of applying the second solder will melt the first. If you have more than a simple soldering job, refer to the books in the Bibliography for more details. Advise your girls to plan simple projects to avoid getting into hard soldering.

For soft soldering you will need: sandpaper or emery cloth, jeweler's file, fine wire, asbestos pad or charcoal block, paste flux, lead coil solder without acid core, tin snips, toothpick or old paint brush, soldering iron or small alcohol blowtorch.

Clean the article to be soldered with an emery cloth and file the pieces that are to be joined. Cut off tiny bits of the solder. Put your two pieces together and bind them with the fine wire. With the toothpick or paint brush, apply flux to the point that is to be soldered. Place the bits of solder along this joint. Apply heat slowly with the blowtorch or iron. Work up to the joint so the metal surrounding it will heat up also. The solder will melt and flow into the joint. The pieces that are to be soldered should always fit tightly together. If they do not, even after binding, they must be held in place with pliers or tongs. After you remove the heat let the joint set undisturbed for a moment until it cools.

If the joint does not solder well, check back through the steps and see what you have been doing wrong. Cleanliness is absolutely important. No joint will solder if there is any dirt or oxidation. When a joint does not solder, the only thing to do is file away all the solder, get it clean and smooth again, and start all over. If you have an article that won't rest flat on an asbestos pad, you can hold it in shape by placing it on a pad of wet newspapers, tissues, or cotton batting. Be sure it is thoroughly wet.

"Do-it-yourself aluminum" requires aluminum solder. Ask at your hardware store about this.

COLD SOLDER is like a glue and comes in a tube. It is applied to both pieces to be joined. The pieces are placed together and clamped or tied until the joint is set. It is useful for some things that are not going to receive much wear. It is more temporary than soft solder. There are many new cold solders and glues on the market which hold very well.

OTHER METHODS. Use rivets, nuts and bolts, sections of metal and slots; lace with wire, or bend edges together. See illustration below.

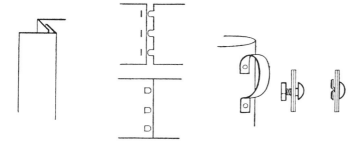

glass

Have you ever seen pictures of the great stained glass windows of the Cathedral of Chartres or the luminous blue windows of Sainte Chappelle? These, or any of the magnificent windows of the Middle Ages, are breathtaking in their beauty. Yet this is only one of the ways that artists have used the medium of glass over the years. Recently we have noticed a great resurgence of interest and work in the stained glass window. Artists such as Matisse have engaged in this form of design, turning out brilliant, startling windows. In this form, glass is usually used for a religious purpose. Glass for everyday use has taken on the essence of art also in the Venetian glass, early European and Irish glass, early American glass, modern Swedish glass, and this country's outstanding contemporary glass manufacturer—Steuben.

The study of the art of glassmaking is another adventure in the hand arts and one that you and your troop may enjoy. The girls can learn something about its history while they are actually doing something with it. There are many techniques in glassmaking that are too advanced for Girl Scouts, yet you will be amazed at the number of handsome articles they can work on without a great deal of skill, cost, or equipment. You can decorate glass items, and you can use plain picture glass or colored glass from bottles. You can often obtain colored glass pieces from companies that manufacture glassware. They will usually supply them to Girl Scouts free of charge or at a nominal fee. Once a Girl Scout troop was given a whole stained glass window from a church that was torn down! Just think of all the wonderful things that they did with it.

In many projects you may have to cut the glass to size. For that reason we include these simple directions. Hold the glass cutter perpendicular to the glass. Mark lines to be cut with ink or hold glass over a piece of paper with the guide line on it. Press and run cutter over the line toward you. Use the same pressure you would use to write darkly with a pencil. Do not scratch the glass. Machine oil or lubricating oil in the cutting wheel helps. Place the handle of the cutter under the glass on the cut line and press gently on each side of the line until glass breaks on the guide line. Move cutter handle up if you are cutting a long line.

THINGS TO MAKE

If the girls are interested in homemaking and decoration, they can make a picture on glass. If they want to record their favorite leaves from a hike, place them under a small piece of glass and paint on a silhouette. If it is a gift-giving occasion, the girls can make small silhouettes of each other and mount them for a gift for their mothers. See illustration. Use black paper to make the silhouette and paste it on or paint it in black paint on the underside of the glass. A backing of white or pale-colored paper and black passe partout (tape) finishes the picture. Small scraps of glass can make a Chinese-like mobile, bound with wire and hung to tinkle in a breeze. Small medallions of colored glass make a very cheery present for hospital patients to hang in their windows. As you and your troop get interested in experimenting in glass, you will happen upon many other uses and ideas.

Glass and plaster

This is a technique for using small pieces of glass. You may use them as they are found or cut them to size.

You will need: heavy twine, pieces of colored glass, mold the size of your finished article, plaster of Paris, wax paper.

You may have a box just the size of your finished article or you may make one by cutting down a milk carton or using various flat cardboard dishes from the grocery. Line the mold with grease or wax paper. The mold should be at least an inch deep. See directions for mixing plaster of Paris on page 80. Place the pieces of glass in the bottom of the mold. You may want to hold them in place with a little glue. Pour the plaster over the glass until it is almost an inch thick. If you want to make a plaque to hang, place a piece of heavy twine or wire about ½ inch from the top in the middle and press the frayed ends into the plaster before it sets. This will be the hanger. You may also make a paperweight by using a mold 2 to 3 inches deep and eliminating the hanger. If you wish the pieces of glass to be transparent, make a border of tin or copper foil about 1 inch wide to go around each piece of glass. Then pour the plaster around the pieces, and to the top of the partitions. Place the hanger as before.

Stained glass

You will need: colored glass scraps, glass cutter, soldering iron, solid wire solder, soldering paste (flux), copper foil, scissors, wire for hook.

Binding

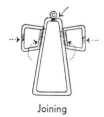

Joining

For a medallion, choose pieces that fit together well and colors that harmonize. To bind each piece of glass, cut a narrow strip of copper foil wide enough to fold over the upper and under side of glass 1/16 of an inch or less. Arrange the pieces in a design. With a toothpick or the end of a match, place a thin coating of flux along the top edge of copper around the glass. Before you start to solder, place an asbestos ironing pad under the medallion. Cut off little chunks of solder and place along the flux (as indicated by arrows). Run hot soldering iron along the copper foil until the solder has melted and gone into the cracks. Run soldering iron completely over the copper to give a smooth silver finish. Repeat soldering on the other side; solder wire hook in place. Let the piece cool thoroughly, scrub with brush and cleansing powder, and hang in a sunny window.

DECORATING GLASS

Etching

The most convenient, safest, and easiest way to etch glass

is with one of the etching creams, such as Amco Glass Etching Cream or Etchall, which can be purchased in art supply stores. There are three general methods—with masking tape, foil, and asphaltum (also used for metal etching). In general these are the materials you will need: glass object, etching cream, sharp knife, spoon or pencil, match or toothpick covered with cotton.

MASKING TAPE METHOD. Clean the glass surface thoroughly and wipe dry with a lint-free cloth. Be careful not to touch or breathe on the portion to be etched. Cover this portion with masking tape. Lap each new strip over the edge of the one before. Now press firmly with the back of a spoon or by rolling a pencil over the tapes.

Trace your design on the tape. Press hard so that the line is clearly indented. With a sharp knife or cutting tool, cut out the design and lift it out. Be sure the knife is sharp so that it will make clean edges. If some of your edges are jagged, trim with a manicure scissors and then lay the tape tight against the glass. Smooth all edges down to the glass so that there are no openings for etching cream to get under.

Squeeze the etching cream directly from the tube onto the openings to be etched. With a match or toothpick wrapped in cotton, spread the cream around so that all portions are covered. Look on the back of the glass to see that no part of the design has been missed. Do not let the cream touch any other part of the glass because the acid starts to work immediately. Let the cream remain two minutes. With a small piece of cardboard scoop up excess cream, then wash remaining cream away under the faucet. Pull off masking tape and your design is etched.

FOIL METHOD. The tape method will make one design, but there are times when you may want the same

design on several pieces of glass or the same monogram on a set of glasses. Then the foil method is the most satisfactory answer because the stencil may be used again. Metal stencil foil which has an adhesive backing can be purchased by the sheet in most art supply stores.

Lay the stencil foil gum side down on a pad of papers and place your design on it with a soft pencil. Cut the foil piece leaving enough border to handle easily, and put it on a sheet of glass or a smooth hard surface to cut out the design. Place the foil design on your glass object (sterile clean) and hold it near a light bulb. The heat softens the adhesive backing and makes it adhere tightly to the glass. Press the foil firmly to the glass with the back of a spoon, making sure all edges of the design are tight against glass. Apply etching cream and proceed as in the first method.

ASPHALTUM METHOD. Draw your design on paper and tape it inside or under the object to be etched. Coat whatever part of the design you don't want etched with black asphaltum or prepared etch control at least 1 inch outside the design. Clean up the edges of the design with a pointed knife, but one that is not sharp enough to scratch the glass. After the asphaltum has been allowed to dry for a few minutes, spread the etching cream onto the parts to be etched with a match or toothpick covered with cotton. Turn to the wrong side to see that all parts have been covered. Proceed with etching as in first method. When all steps have been completed, remove the asphaltum with turpentine. The advantages of this method are that it allows for a freer design without the characteristic channel lines of a stencil. Some ideas for etched glass and how to make negative or positive designs are shown below.

64

Painting

There are many items in glass that can be made into handsome gifts with a painted decoration. Of course there are many pieces of glass that are better left clear, too, but this is a choice you must make for yourself.

Painted Stiegel glass

There are many items, such as jars, bottles, and glass bricks, that can be decorated with regular oil paints or enamels and the design given a coat of varnish and the colors will last. For those items that are subjected to harder usage and must be washed often, it is wise to use one of the glass paints that are oven set such as Dek-All. Whatever paint you use, follow the same procedure with the exception of the oven setting. Only those paints which so specify on the bottle should be oven set. The time required differs with the brand of paint, so refer to the label.

Make a pattern the size of your glass if you are not going to paint freehand. Slip the pattern inside the glass and fasten with tape. Some glasses curve at the bottom. If so, you will need to make slits and lap over the bottom edge into little darts as shown. Clean the glass with a standard cleaning fluid or the solvent of the paints you are using. Wipe with a lint-free cloth. Keep fingers and breath off the glass because a sterile clean surface is necessary for good results. Stir paints well. Use a soft brush with a fine point. Mix paints until they flow freely and evenly. Fill in all parts with one color, allow that to dry, then fill in another color. Dry the piece about twenty-four hours. Set paint by baking in an oven. Place the article in a cold oven, bring it to the heat required in the directions, and hold it there for the time specified. Turn off the oven and let the glass cool before removing it. If you have applied an extra heavy coat, let it remain hot a little longer. The ordinary heat and time is about 15 minutes at 300° F.

Remember, paint only glass that will be improved by decoration. This usually means inexpensive glass. Some pieces of glass would be ruined by any painted design no matter how well applied. Keep the design simple. Just lines suggested by the brush strokes are often the most effective.

Reverse painting

Painting in reverse on glass is an art which dates back to Roman antiquity. It has sometimes been classed with

65

painting in general and at other times found its place among the craftsmen working in gold, silver, and jewels. The basic method has changed little over the years.

Small round pieces may be used as coasters, a design painted on glass may be framed with wood or simply framed by binding with passe partout and used as a wall decoration. The simple silhouette mentioned earlier is a good project for a beginner. In addition, a heavy glass panel could be framed in wood and used as a tray, or you can use glass in combination with many decorative objects and pieces of furniture.

You will need: water colors, oils, or tempera; background color in enamel, gold or silver leaf, varnish, brush, newspapers, glass the size of your object, small fine pointed brushes, larger flat brush to apply background color.

Place your design on paper the size of the glass. Tape this face down on the front of the glass. Turn the glass over and paint, beginning with the highlights and ending with the background. Experiment first on a piece of scrap glass because it is a little hard to get used to the idea of putting the shadings in first. Your finished design will be the reverse of the drawing so be sure that all lettering is in reverse on the wrong side. You may also paint directly on the glass without the design underneath. Keep the first designs very simple.

After the design is painted on the glass, let it dry for twenty-four hours. Paint background (or apply gold leaf), let it dry thoroughly, and finish with a coat of enamel.

Finished Picture

Gold leaf on glass

Gold leaf on glass was once a widely used art but now seems fairly extinct. It is a very interesting craft, used alone or in connection with painting in reverse, and is really not too difficult to do. Its uses are similar to reverse painting. There is also other metal leaf, cheaper than real gold, yet resembling it in appearance. Or you may use silver leaf.

You will need: drawing pen, black ink, gold leaf, gold leaf brush, called "tipper"—all available in art supply stores—small paint brush, sizing solution (made by adding pinch of gelatin to ⅔ cup boiling water), ruler, flat black paint, turpentine, background paint.

1. Place design under glass, ink in outline on right side. Let dry. Turn glass to wrong side, clean carefully. Gold leaf will go on this side.

2. Paint the part of the design to be gold with sizing solution, keeping inside the inked outlines.

3. Electrify tipper by brushing over your hair. Touch to leaf to lift it, and put it over the spot you wet with sizing solution. Wrinkles will not show on finished work. Keep placing piece of gold next to each other until design is covered. Don't try to straighten them.

4. Tilt glass, dry it ten to fifteen minutes.

5. Place glass over a light bulb so inked detail will show through gold leaf.

6. With wooden point, etch design on the gold leaf, and redraw outlines where gold has extended over inked lines.

7. Lay glass flat with the gold-leaf side up. With black paint thinned a little with turpentine, paint over the gold design to fasten it and to protect the gold leaf.

8. Let it dry, rub off excess gold leaf with damp cloth. Wash off ink design on front. Paint the background, going over the gold leaf. Use two coats if needed. Use ruler to make straight lines.

Gold leaf can also be used on metal, paper, or wood. You can decorate trays, illuminated manuscripts, and furniture. On these materials, draw the design lightly in pencil, then follow steps 2, 3, and 6. Rub off excess gold after it is dry, and give the article a coat of varnish.

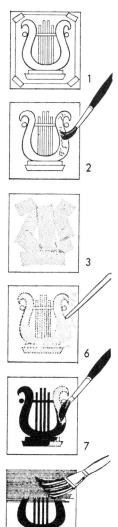

leather

Many good-looking items can be made from leather without much difficulty or cost. However, as the leader, you need to know a few more things about leathermaking than about some of the other arts because some projects are too expensive and technical for beginners.

It is best to start with leather scraps, which can often be had for the asking from leathergoods manufacturers or purchased by the pound from arts and crafts supply houses. The scraps range anywhere from 2 inches square to 6 x 8 inches. The projects that you and the girls work on would have to be fairly small, but there is a great opportunity to use imagination in the artful combining of leathers, or leather and fabric, embroidery, etc. The buckles, purse, painted and appliqued lapel pins shown are some suggestions.

As you work, talk about all the items you use every day that are made of leather. Examine the way they are made, the designs used, the way they are put together. In this way the girls will come to an appreciation of the material and learn more about their own projects. Since scrap leather can be cut with ordinary scissors, the only real techniques you need to know are the ways of joining —gluing, sewing, lacing

If you find a piece among the scraps that retains a finger-nail mark when you press on the edge, it is probably tool-

68

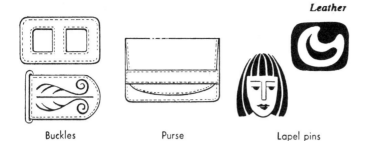

Buckles   Purse   Lapel pins

ing leather. This leather, which comes in a variety of colors, has been specially prepared to retain impressions made on the surface with tools or stamps. Save such pieces because they take a design beautifully.

If there is no way for you to get scrap leather or leather skins, or even a chamois or old leather jacket, it is much better that your troop work in another art before resorting to any of the kit projects now on the market. Many people resort to these prepunched, precut, predesigned wallets, belts, or shoe kits when they can't find scraps immediately. These kits give the girls nothing, absolutely nothing, in the way of creative achievement, satisfaction, skills, or appreciation—all the things arts and crafts should give them. These kits cannot and should not be considered part of a Girl Scout program and may not be used to fulfill any badge requirements.

Start on a simple level—this is important. Inspire your girls to use their imaginations. Let the girls take a few pieces of leather home and make something imaginative. When they bring the articles in the next week, you will be amazed at the remarkable array. The items may be crooked and not quite hold together, but they certainly will be imaginative.

This chapter gives the steps in the various techniques used in working with leather. Scan them first to see what the possibilities are and, when the girls decide what they want to make, read the section on that project more carefully. If Suzy wants to make a coin purse, you'll need to know how to cut and sew it and how to apply some type of fastening—a snap, slot, button, or some other arrangement. If Cecelia wants to make tooled buttons, tooling is what you would look up. If Jean wants to make a decorated case for glasses, you need to find out how to decorate leather. So, you see, each project has its own special techniques, but only a rare one needs them all.

69

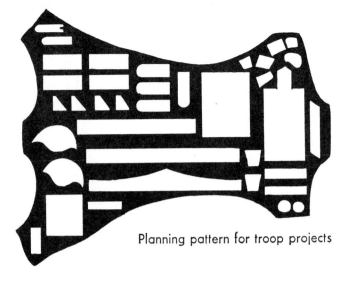

Planning pattern for troop projects

and from arts and crafts companies. Look in a current
purchased in art supply stores, sometimes in luggage shops,
buy a larger skin or two smaller ones. Leather may be

When you are ready to progress to more difficult tasks,
remember that good leather skins are expensive and that
a carefully drawn plan is important. A difficult project
should be made in muslin first. The cost will be less per
girl if a group gets together and buys a skin, figuring each
inch closely. For example, you can buy a skin 2 x 3 feet,
but before you buy, use a piece of brown paper to see
if you can get each girl's pattern on it. You may have to
art magazine for the names of leather dealers.

If colored leather is desired, it is best to buy it in the
color you wish. Only small pieces of light-colored leather
can be dyed. Craft supply houses carry a number of
leather dyes. Among these are quick-drying enamels, lac-
quers, waterproof inks, alcohol- and water-soluble dyes.
The directions for use are supplied. Use color with restraint
and be sure the leather is absolutely clean and free of
grease before you start.

There are various kinds of leathers:

TAILORING LEATHER. This includes any hide normally
tanned—calf, sheepskin, pigskin, cowhide. It comes in
various weights and should be selected according to the
article you wish to make.

TOOLING LEATHER. This is the only leather suitable
for pressed-in decoration. Calf is suitable for soft articles;
cowhide for stamped designs and heavier projects such
as belts.

70

SUEDE. This leather has one smooth side and one soft, furry side. It may be used for gloves, slippers, soft purses. Some suedes are thin enough for lining.

LINING LEATHERS. These thin leathers, some smooth, others suede, come in a variety of colors and should be bought with a specific project in mind. Sometimes they are called skivers.

LEATHER PROCESSES

Here are the tools you need for working with leathers: paper patterns; tailor's chalk or pointed crayon; steel ruler; razor or sharp knife (skiving knife or paring knife sharpened along one side), or sharp shears or tin snips; piece of heavy glass, marble or smooth hardwood; glue (see page 76); paste wax; pencil or ball-point pen; waterproof ink; shellac; sandpaper; modeler; plus any special tools required for each decorating process.

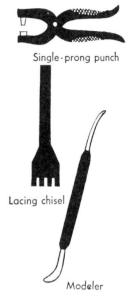

Single-prong punch

Lacing chisel

Modeler

Working with leather differs somewhat from other arts in that you decorate *before* you assemble it rather than afterward. For that reason we have outlined the leather processes in the order in which you would use them.

Cutting

Once you have planned your structural and decorative design, lay your pattern on the wrong side of the leather. Draw carefully around it with chalk, crayon, or ball-point pen. Lay the pattern on the leather to waste as little leather as possible, yet not getting too close to the grainy edges or to scars and holes. With your knife or shears cut along the guide lines, using the steel ruler to keep edges straight. Cut all corners accurately and be sure the knife is sharp enough to avoid fuzzy edges. After all the pieces are cut out, assemble them and correct any spot that needs it.

Skiving

Some leathers are so thick that putting the edges together forms too heavy a seam. On these pieces you need to skive (thin) the leather at the edge with a skiving knife or a paring knife sharpened along one edge. With the leather right side down on the glass, marble, or wood slab, hold the skiving knife away from you (as shown) and almost parallel to the leather. Hold your hand on the leather

between body and the knife to prevent the leather from slipping. It makes the job easier if you wet the leather slightly before cutting. Slice away small slivers of the leather until your edge is thinned down gradually. It takes practice to produce an evenly skived edge so *proceed with caution.* Sandpapering afterward will help give you an even edge. Skiving is to be used only where the leather is so thick it would make awkward seams.

DECORATING LEATHER

The process of decorating the leather comes next, even though you have decided before purchasing it what type of decoration to use. Decoration should be used only where it becomes a structural part of the design and then used with restraint, and it should be geared to the size, weight, and future use of the object.

Tooling

You will need: your design on paper, tooling leather, sponge or soft cloth, modeler or nut pick, piece of glass or hardwood, ruler or French curve.

PLACING THE DESIGN. Turn the leather to the wrong side and dampen until dark spots appear on the right side. Always dampen the entire surface, not just the part which is to receive the design. Turn the leather over and place the paper design over the area to be tooled. The outer edges of leather should be included in the design so that it is properly proportioned within the area. Your design should be a pleasing combination of straight or gently curving lines with the areas marked that are to be laid down for background. Keep the design simple and not too realistic. Go over the lines of the design with the modeler or nut pick. Do not tear through the design. You will find that it does not take much pressure. Be careful not to lean your hands, watches, or rings on the leather when it is wet because every impression will remain. Draw as many lines as you can with a ruler or French curve to keep them clean and free of faltering or wavering.

After the entire design has been traced, remove the paper and the lines will be indented into the surface of the leather as a guide to the tooling. Leather is placed on a hard surface (the marble, glass, or hardwood slab). The

72

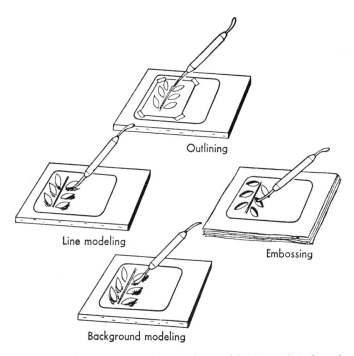

Outlining

Line modeling

Embossing

Background modeling

next step is to go over these lines with the pointed end of a modeler (nut pick or pointed wooden stick) and deepen all the impressions in the design. If water oozes when you press down on the tool, the leather is too wet and should be allowed to dry for a while. Leather that is too wet wrinkles when you work on it. If it has changed to a lighter color, it is too dry and must be wet again from the back. Experience will teach you how to tell from color and feel when the leather is just right.

MODELING. The general method of producing the design is the modeling technique. Although there are several tools you can buy and use in all these processes, we refer to the one which is illustrated. Place your leather right side up on the glass or hardwood. Decide which area of your design is to be raised. With spoon end of the modeler pointed to the higher part, press down the leather around the outlines of the design. The greatest pressure comes just outside the lines and gradually slopes up to edges from there. Work around the entire design this way, lowering the background just beyond the design lines. If the raised portions need to be modeled or lines drawn deeper, do this with the other end of the modeler. Numerous light

73

strokes are better for modeling than a few heavy strokes.

EMBOSSING OR REPOUSSÉ. This is a tooling technique in which one part of the design is definitely raised away from the original surface of the leather. Do the modeling around the design as described above, then turn the leather over to the wrong side on a piece of felt or cotton batting and with the modeler gently work over the part that is to be raised. The design lines will show on the back if modeled deep enough. Do the embossing gingerly and with restraint because once the leather has been stretched it cannot be shrunk back into shape. The design should not be raised too high. This raised portion must be supported. Fill the hollows with plastic wood, or sawdust, cotton, or kapok mixed with glue. To keep this filling in place, glue thin paper or leather over it.

With the right side facing you, model around the edges of the design. If you wish a stippled background, go over it with the modeler, making scattered dots.

Carving

The next two techniques involve cutting through the surface of the leather. Examples of this type of work are the carved leather saddles of the West. Carving is particularly adaptable to cowhide but, with care and restraint, can be used in combination with tooling or tooling calf.

INCISING. Incising is the process of cutting straight lines into leather. Prepare the leather as for tooling, dampening from the back and tracing on the lines. Your tool can be an incising knife, razor, or stencil knife but should be thin and very sharp. Use a straightedge as a guide when making your cuts on the indented lines. Hold the knife to make a clean perpendicular cut, and cut through ¼ of the thickness of the leather—never more than ½. Corners are apt to fray, so avoid this by not quite closing your cutting lines at a corner—leave about 1/16 inch between lines. It will help make your work more exact if you keep your leather evenly damp with a sponge and sharpen your knife regularly with an oilstone. Open the incised lines with the side of the modeler's foot and work down the background on either side of the lines by modeling. You may also combine incising with stamping by stamping down the background instead of modeling.

74

STAMPING. Some designs may call for a background with design. The method of applying this design is called stamping. For this you may use a variety of articles filed down to a blunt point, such as a small nail, knitting needles, mechanical pencil with lead removed, or small dowels or regular stamping tools. You also need a mallet and scrap pieces of leather.

Small, closely spaced depressions may be made on the leather for background treatment with the type of objects mentioned above. Try out different objects and spacings on scrap leather first. Hold the stamping tool perpendicular and tap squarely with the mallet. A helter-skelter effect is better than having the depressions in rows or patterns. Do not try to go over a stamped design; the result is almost always messy. Practice until you have an even pressure at each blow of the mallet and then place the design on your good piece. As in tooling, the leather must be damp.

General hints

Roll leather right side out to avoid graining.

Never close damp leather in a box or a cupboard because it may mold.

Mistakes in tooling can seldom be erased. With the flat end of the modeler, work over the mistake, first on the front and then on the back. If leather is cut through while incising, paste thin leather or fabric on the back to reinforce it. Then handle gently. If a nick has been taken out of the leather surface, glue the rough places back and retool when the leather has dried.

Keep hands clean, do not touch your face and then the leather—the slightest trace of oil from the skin will leave a stain on unglazed leather. Sometimes the metal tools will tend to darken the light-colored leather. To diminish this effect, work with the leather not too wet, and put only light pressure on the tool.

Combinations

You can combine leather with leathers of different weight and color, or with fabrics, embroidery, or metal. A tooled leather belt, for example, is handsome with a plain copper or brass buckle. Experiment with such metal items as nail-

heads, small rivets, eyelets, and polished brass paper fasteners, small plain metal buttons, wire, old coins, etc. These items should be well spaced, carefully planned for, integrated with the design, and used sparingly. Imagination is always geared by good taste. When you are decorating with paper fasteners, line the piece with fabric or thin leather to cover the metal shanks. Clear nail polish over the metal fasteners' heads will keep them bright. The belt fob shows a combination of several decorating techniques and brass rivets.

ASSEMBLING

Before you lace or stitch the pieces together, be sure the edges are straight and smooth. If a razor blade fails to make roughened edges neat, rub them with very fine sandpaper. If the leather is too soft, stiffen it first by touching along the edges with shellac; then when it is dry, sand lightly. If the cut edge is lighter than the leather, it can be touched up with dye or waterproof ink. Then the edges should be beveled slightly with the modeler. If several layers are used, or a few thick pieces of leather come together, the edges may be further finished by rubbing wax into them until they are smooth. On lightweight or suede leathers these treatments are unnecessary since the edge is thin.

Gluing

You may use one of the specially prepared leather glues such as three-in-one leather glue or Higgins vegetable glue. Vegetable glue is a rather heavy adhesive and should be applied with a short-bristled stiff brush. (If the glue is too thick, thin it with water.) A satisfactory glue that you can make yourself is rye flour paste. It spreads easily and may be put on with a small brush. Spread the glue to a smooth film. If you are gluing a seam, brush the glue on ¼ inch of the edge of each piece; if it is a lining, place glue over the entire surface of each piece.

RYE FLOUR PASTE

2 tablespoons rye flour	1 cup water
¼ teaspoon alum	Few drops cil of cloves

Mix flour, alum, and enough water to make smooth cream. Add remaining water, cook over low heat until it is like thin white sauce and is translucent. Long, slow cooking increases stickiness. Remove from stove and add oil of cloves. The mixture can be kept for a year in a closed jar in refrigerator. (Cloves prevent the paste from spoiling.)

Sewing

Leather articles that look most professional are stitched. If the leather is not too thick, stitching may be done on a sewing machine but more often it should be done by hand.

You will need smooth strong thread of several ply (buttonhole twist, shoe twist, or linen or some of the crochet cottons), pad of newspapers, awl or coarse needle, ruler.

Stitching should be about 1/16 inch from the edge and 8-10 stitches per inch for thin leathers, ⅛ inch from the edge and 5-6 stitches per inch for heavier leathers. Use a thread appropriate to the weight of the leathers. You will need to mark the stitches for sewing and punch each one through with an awl, coarse needle, or a sewing machine. Place a guide line the desired distance from the edge and with a ruler and awl on a pad of newspapers, mark with light dots evenly spaced; then punch them through with your sharp instrument.

If you use a sewing machine, change the ordinary sewing needle to a heavy-duty needle. Set the stitch regulator to the desired number of stitches, place the leather under the needle with a piece of paper under the leather. Work the machine by hand, turning the wheel for each stitch. This will give you evenly spaced holes. If you let the machine go, the stitches will be closer together at thick spots and farther apart at thinner spots because the leather is not of equal thickness. That is why it is necessary to do each hole by hand.

SADDLE STITCH. This stitch uses two needles. Thread each needle with a convenient length to use. Knot two ends together. Work in and out stitch, both needles going through the total thickness of the seam in the same holes in opposite directions as shown. When stitching is completed, go between layers, put a spot of glue on end of thread, and fasten to inside.

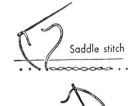

Saddle stitch

Back stitch

BACK STITCH. As in all hand stitching, holes are

77

punched before stitching. Other than this, the stitch is the same back stitch used in all sewing. See illustration.

GENERAL HINTS. Always use a needle that is coarse enough for the thread used. Use a thimble. If the needle is hard to pull through, a small pair of pliers may be used. Tangling can be prevented by running the thread over a piece of wax. Start stitching on the seam but never at a corner.

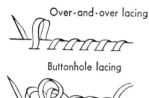

Over-and-over lacing

Buttonhole lacing

Lacing

Any worth-while laced project deserves real leather lacing. Other materials may crack and split. See illustration for two simple lacing stitches.

Punch holes with slit punch or revolving punch.

Fittings

There are various articles that require snap buttons, eyelets, buckles, rings, and other fittings. Nearly all of them require a special tool to put them onto your leather article (see illustration). The fittings and the tools for applying them are purchased through arts and crafts supply stores. Inquire about the use of these tools when buying them. You will also find an explanation of these tools in the books listed in the Bibliography.

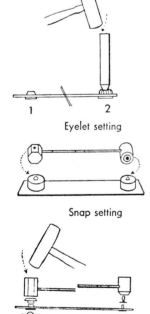

1   2

Eyelet setting

Snap setting

Finishing

All smooth leathers benefit from good saddle soaping. Use very little water with the soap. Polish with a soft cloth. To give the leather a protective coat, apply a little paste wax sparingly. Put the wax between the layers of the polishing cloth; it will prevent any wax from getting into corners and crevices. Suede may be given a fresh appearance by rubbing with a small piece of the same leather, or rubbing very lightly with a fine sandpaper. Any effort you make to preserve and keep the surface of your leatherwork clean will reward you.

clay

For the youngest Brownie clay can be a source of utmost delight, and for the most sophisticated Senior it can assume the dignity of true art. There are many qualities and grades of clay that are used for different kinds of ware. At first just experiment or play. Let the girls roll, squeeze, and push the clay, make it into snakes or balls or snowman-like figures, and probably put it back in the bin at the end of the troop meetings. After this, when you have helped the girls gain some appreciation of clay through pictures and/or examples of articles made by different techniques in clay, they will want to make a finished article.

Real clay must be fired (baked) in a kiln. Certain techniques must be followed to make a piece that will not blow up in the kiln. Before you start, check to see if a school, college, china factory, or community center in your town will let you use its kiln. It is so discouraging for a girl to have made a lovely item she wants to preserve only to fir that she can't get it fired. If you cannot make arrangements to use a kiln, then use self-hardening clay or oven-firing clay. On this type of clay you may paint the decoration. Remember, however, it will not produce the same beauty and permanence as real clay.

When the girls are ready for advanced techniques, they can try digging and straining their own clay. Some of the books listed in the Bibliography will tell you more about this and other advanced techniques.

CARE AND PREPARATION OF CLAY

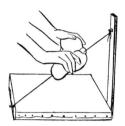

Clay must be moist to be usable. For comparatively small amounts, put it in a biscuit tin (painted on the inside to prevent rust). Line the box with a moistened sack or cloth and put a damp cloth over the clay to give added protection.

Clay needs to be well beaten or wedged so that no airholes or lumps remain to cause the work to explode while firing. One method is to raise a lump of clay over the head and then bang it on the table. On a wedging board, cut the section in half and bang each section again. When you cut it in half and no airholes appear, the clay is ready to use. Clay can be pushed, banged, kneaded, and pulled, but should not be allowed to dry out. Keep the fingers slightly damp with a sponge.

GENERAL MATERIALS AND TOOLS

One of the advantages of working with clay is that you need so few tools. Here is a suggested list of materials.

Clay, water, glaze or paint and shellac.

Work bat of plaster. Use a greased pie or cake tin or cardboard box for a mold. Add plaster to water until it is like thick cream. When water has absorbed all it can, the plaster will appear in little mountains on the surface of the water. A good way to mix it is in a plastic bag or rubber bowl. Never pour any of the mixture down the sink. Pour into a mold, dry, and use as a base for wedging. Dry the bat after each use by placing near heat.

Tin cans or old pails for water, paints, etc.

Piece of oilcloth for the worktable or bench.

Sponge.

Cardboard template (see page 82).

Fine sandpaper to smooth hardened work.

Knife.

Modeling tools, which can be purchased; or tongue depressors, nut picks, or orange sticks.

Two biscuit tins—one for bulk clay and one for unfinished work.

Cloths to place over unfinished work.

80

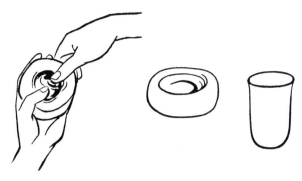

METHODS

Pinch pot method

Pinch pots or bowls are easily made from a piece of clay which, after wedging, is carefully worked into a ball that fits in the hand. Actually the name is somewhat of a misnomer for it is a rotating motion not a pinching one. By gradually increasing the pressure in the center of the piece with the thumbs and turning the ball, the clay begins to take shape. Simple and interesting contours can be made. Be careful to see that the walls are of even thickness all the way around and at the base.

Coil method

Pat or roll clay to ¼-inch thickness and cut out a flat base of the desired size. You can use an inverted tumbler or a compass to make a round base. Now begin to build the sides. Roll a small wad of clay into a coil the thickness of the wall desired, probably about ¼ inch. Roll as quickly as possible from quite soft clay. Start laying the coils on the base. To join the coils, make a diagonal cut at each end of the coil to make the ends fit smoothly together.

The shape is changed by the position of the clay on top of the last layer. The work may be swelled outward by placing the new coil slightly to the outside of the one beneath it, or it may be curved in by placing the new coil a little to the inside. As each coil is laid, weld it to the last. Place the coils so they do not end directly on top of one another. When three or four coils have been laid, smooth them into the others while the clay is still soft. You can smooth the clay with the fingers, knife blade, or modeling tool, or you may leave the coils as they are.

MAKING A TEMPLATE. A template is used as a guide to keep the vase or bowl even on all sides. First make a profile drawing of the vase or bowl you are making. Draw it a little larger than the size of your final piece. Make the template by tracing one side of the drawing on a piece of cardboard and cutting along the line showing the shape of the pot. This gives you a template of the same shape as the outside contour of the pot.

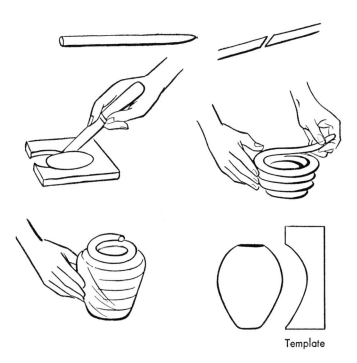

Template

Slab method

In addition to the materials listed on page 80, you will need a wooden board 18 x 12 inches, several strips of wood 18 inches long and ½ inch thick, rolling pin or length of broom handle.

Cover the board with cloth, brown paper, or oilcloth to prevent sticking. Nail strips of wood to the board after you decide on the size of the clay slab. The thickness of the slab is determined by the height of the strips, in this case ½ inch. Wedge or knead the clay, then press it firmly into the board. Roll with rolling pin until smooth.

If you are making tiles, let the clay dry slightly before

removing the strips. Cut tiles the size you want (5 x 5 inches is a good size). Then finish drying in a cool place. Edges dry more quickly so they should be dampened from time to time to make the drying even. To make a firmer tile, mix in some grog with the clay. Grog is finely ground powder made from fired pieces. To make a box or pitcher, use the slab when it is still fairly soft. Make patterns for the several pieces you need. For example, make four sides, bottom, top, and inside top for a box. Bottom pieces always fit inside the side pieces. Lay the pattern on the slab and cut out the shapes with a sharp knife. If the knife sticks or pulls the clay out of shape, the clay is too wet.

To join the pieces, roughen the edges and apply a little clay mixed with water to the consistency of thick cream.

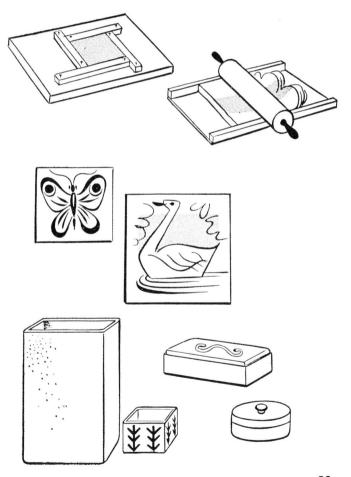

This mixture is called slip. Press the edges together and finish. Join by cementing the inside of the corner with wet clay. Strengthen the outside corners by dipping your fingers in clay slip and rubbing the outside of each corner.

When the clay is leather-hard (firm but still damp), smooth the surface by rubbing with fine sandpaper. Then, after complete drying, add the decoration.

Sculpturing method*

This method of working in clay produces excellent results and is really very simple to do. The principle is to work from a square or rectangle and cut away the clay until the design pleases you. For example, to make a free-form bowl, start to work on the bottom, cutting away until you have a shape that satisfies you. Let it dry slightly, turn over carefully, and hollow out the inside to make a bowl shape. Work until all the walls are even. You can use this same method of carving for modeling small figures.

You may want to try some of this sculpture in plaster of Paris first. The directions for mixing plaster are on page 80. Use a cut-down milk carton for your mold, and try your design by cutting into a rectangle of plaster of Paris with a knife.

Modeling method

Your imagination and feeling for form can be given full reign when modeling in clay. Forms should have interesting design from all sides. Animals or people may suggest forms to you, but don't try to make them too realistic. Decide on a basic shape and start with a piece of clay that shape. It's fun to start with such simple forms as balls, cones, larger rolls, or slabs and proceed from there to more interesting shapes. When the object is completed, set it aside to harden. Solid objects need small hollows in the base to prevent them from cracking in the kiln. Smooth the surfaces with a damp sponge. Dry thoroughly and rub the surface with fine sandpaper before firing. Larger figures require wire frames or armatures. Ask about these at your art supply store.

---

* The author wishes to make acknowledgment to Miss Edris Eckhart, Cleveland, Ohio, for this method.

DECORATING CLAY

Clay can be decorated in many effective ways. After you have read about the various types, decide which method is adaptable or suitable to the piece you have in mind.

Incised design

By using a knife or other sharp instrument and actually cutting your design into the unfired, leather-hard clay, you can create an incised decoration. You can make it just a line design or you can bring the design out in relief by cutting away part of the background. Pieces should then be fired, glaze applied, and fired again.

Sgraffito

Sgraffito is an Italian word meaning scratch. To make a sgraffito decoration, cover the whole piece with a coating of a contrasting colored slip. Then form the design by carefully carving or scratching through the outer slip and exposing some of the clay beneath. The slip should be painted on leather-hard, unfired clay. The slip may be applied by any of the methods for applying glaze described on page 87. The design may be lightly sketched with a pencil first. The carving is usually done with a modeling tool or sharp-edged instrument. During the carving process, keep the clay in leather-hard condition. The finished piece is dried, fired once, glazed with a transparent glaze, and then fired again.

Embossed designs

Embossed designs are those which are added to the original piece. They may take nearly any form you wish but should usually be less than ¼-inch thick.

The original piece is completed and allowed to dry until it is slightly softer than leather-hard. The embossed designs should be modeled in soft, fresh clay. Lay the designs on in little pieces and work them into the background. Water smooths the clay very easily, but use it sparingly so the original piece will not soften and lose its shape. It is helpful to make a paper pattern first and cut out the embossed designs with a knife. By using your imagination you can create many unusual designs. Fire the ware once, glaze, and fire again. The first firing is called bisque, the second is glost.

Slip decoration

Slip decoration is painting the ware with ground clay thinned to paint consistency. Slip, which is light or white in color, can be used effectively against a dark background. Or, light-colored slip can be tinted by adding metallic oxides, stains, or underglaze colors. Slip is usually applied to leather-hard pieces. It is bisque fired, glazed with transparent or light glaze, and fired again.

Glaze

Glaze is the usual decoration for pottery. It is described on pages 86-88.

Painted unfired ware

Indian-type pottery may be painted when thoroughly dry with a design in tempera paints and covered with a coat of shellac. The inside can be coated with shellac or hot paraffin.

Of course you can always leave your piece plain and merely give the surface a polish with a stone or the side of a pencil.

GLAZING

Glass is the principal ingredient in the glazes used on pottery ware. When the pottery is fired, the glaze melts and forms a glassy coating over the clay. Glazes may be purchased in powdered form and mixed with water to prepare them for application.

There are many different kinds of glazes that may be purchased from a local craft supply dealer. The dealer will give you complete instructions for applying and firing. Be sure to find out at what temperature the glaze fires.

Types of glazes

SIMPLE GLAZING. Giving a piece of pottery a coat of transparent or colored glaze gives lovely all-over coloring. It is applied to the ware after the latter has been given a first or bisque firing.

86

UNDERGLAZE PAINTING. This means painting a design on pottery with special underglaze colors after a bisque firing. Then a light coating of transparent glaze is applied and the ware fired again. The second firing, known as glost firing, gives life and brilliance and protects ware against moisture.

OVERGLAZE PAINTING. This is sometimes called enamel or china painting and is generally used only for fine pieces of pottery. The ware is given a bisque firing, a clear glaze, and a glost firing. The designs are then painted on

Applying glazes

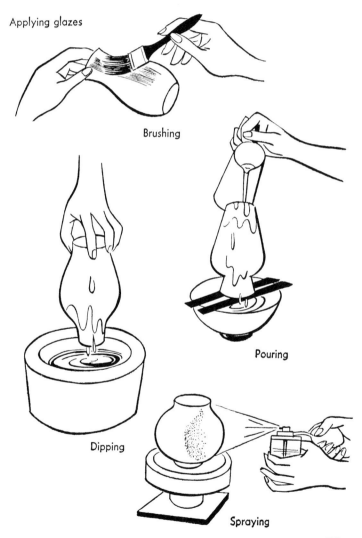

Brushing

Pouring

Dipping

Spraying

87

with special overglaze colors or enamels, and the colors hardened by a third firing at lower heat than the previous two.

Applying glazes

Pieces have one firing before applying glaze. In this state, pottery must be kept very clean. If any grease or dirt gets on it, glaze will not stick.

BRUSHING. This method may be used with practically any type of ware. Use a soft, flat brush dipped into glaze, and give the piece two or three coats. Brush in one direction only. Always remember to wipe bottom before firing.

POURING. To apply to the inside, fill the piece half-full with glaze, tilt, and turn until the inside surface is coated. Pour out excess.

To glaze the outside, place piece on two parallel sticks across pan, put glaze in a cup or saucepan and pour over the piece, letting it run down until all sides are covered.

DIPPING. Put glaze in a pan. Holding piece by rim or base, dip into glaze. Place upside down on two parallel sticks across container so excess may drain off.

SPRAYING. Use a special spray obtained from a pottery supply dealer. Place piece on modeling wheel and revolve while glaze is being sprayed. This is the most difficult method and should be reserved for advanced work.

Touch up spots where pieces have been held with a soft brush dipped in glaze. Allow glaze to dry thoroughly before touching.

Many glazes contain lead, so be sure any girl who has a cut on her hand does not get any glaze near the cut.

FIRING AND KILNS

Firing is the baking of the pottery to make the pieces durable and waterproof, and to set glaze. It is done in special oven-like kilns, which may be electric, gas, oil burning, or homemade. Commercial kilns come in many sizes and types.

If you take your wares to a commercial kiln, be sure to tell them what temperature your clay and glaze should be fired. To transport glazed pottery to the kiln without injuring it, place the pieces in a deep box, separating them with cardboard partitions so they cannot rub against one another.

The primitive kiln also offers a solution to the problem of firing, but only in part, for the second or glost firing is not satisfactory in this type of kiln. Nevertheless, one firing is much better than none, and saves many pieces which might otherwise be lost.

All clay must be absolutely dry before placing in kiln. Damp clay explodes in firing. All cracks and crevices must be mended with slip, and dried before firing.

Primitive kiln

There are many varieties of outdoor kilns. Many camps have a favorite type. This is only one of many.

Dig a pit in the ground, place small pieces of wood, bark, and dry grass on the bottom, light and burn until there is a bed of live coals. Place pottery pieces to be fired (first dried in sun) in an iron or clay kettle, large pieces on bottom, small ones on top. Cover the kettle loosely so that moisture may evaporate. Put the kettle into pit. Place bark, wood, and grass on top of the kettle, and burn from five to eight hours. Allow the fire to die down slowly. When the kettle is cool, remove the pottery.

textile arts and needlework

Weaving, embroidery, rug hooking—these are among the traditional arts of the homemaker and as such should have an important place in the Girl Scout program. There is a wide choice of activities for the troop that works in this medium. The girls can make articles to wear—a woven belt, a printed kerchief, or an embroidered decoration on a blouse. Or they can make a number of household articles.

Because these arts are more familiar to women than some of the other arts, there is perhaps more tendency to have already designed products or patterns for the girls to copy or merely fill-in. There is such an abundance of mediocre stamped patterns available in embroidery, rug hooking, and needlepoint, that the natural tendency is to use this easier way. However, it is just as important, if not more so, to allow the girls to be creative in this field; to design their own; to use their ideas, releasing their potential personal growth.

As in all the arts, start on a project small and simple enough to avoid discouragement and provide enjoyment.

WEAVING

Weaving, one of the earliest of the home arts, arose from need. However, it was not long before man saw beyond the mere utility of fabric and wanted beauty too. Color

90

and design were added and it soon became an art. Hand looming gives a satisfaction and a richness of design that machine weaving can never quite capture.

The steps we have chosen here are the beginning ones, but they all lead to more advanced procedures. To be able to say you have really learned to weave you must have made something on a regular table loom. There are many types of looms. Many books on weaving show different kinds of looms that can be easily constructed.

One simple way to start learning the art of weaving is the over-and-under weaving of strips of colored construction paper to make a paper mat. Next try making a pot holder from loopers. This stage should not last long, however, and is best suited to the young child. Soon you should move on to the first steps in learning to appreciate craftsmanship by helping the girls actually create their own designs.

The cardboard loom

On the cardboard loom you can make many small articles. Purses, bookmarks, book covers are only a few of the possibilities. The principle is simple enough for the beginner yet it is still possible to carry out elaborate ideas and designs on these looms to exercise your creative abilities. The method of setting up the loom and weaving described below is specifically for a purse.

You will need: woolen, silk, cotton or linen yarns, cardboard loom, heavy needle.

SETTING UP THE LOOM. Cut two pieces of cardboard the exact size you wish to make your purse and paste them together. This double thickness will make your loom stronger. Paste cellophane tape over the top where the pins are to go. Place an even number of pins about ⅛-¼ inch apart, according to the thickness of the yarn. Use a pencil and ruler to make sure the pins are evenly spaced. The warp threads are the tight lengthwise threads that are the foundation of the work. The woof threads (also called "weft") are the cross-wise threads that weave over and under the foundation. With a pin fasten one end of the wrap thread 1 inch from the top left. Then take the thread up and around the first pin, going from the left to the right, carry it to the bottom of the loom and up again on the other side, hooking it over

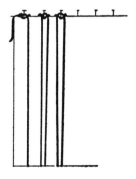

the same pin again from left to right. Bring the thread down the back, and up the front around the second pin; down the front, up the back around the same pin. Continue until all the pins are wound. End by pinning the warp to the right side of the loom placing the pin about 1 inch from the top as on the other side.

WEAVING THE FABRIC. Thread your woof thread into a very long needle or cardboard shuttle and begin weaving at the lower right-hand corner of your loom and continue until you are all the way across. Then turn your loom over and weave again until you are back where you started. Continue weaving around and around until the project is completed. Keep the warp threads straight with your needle and beat down the woof threads with a comb. You can join a new piece of thread by just leaving a long enough end in the center of the cardboard and weaving it in when the work is completed.

If you wish to make a book cover, bookmark, or place mat, you weave on only one side of the loom. The warp threads are wound on pins placed at top *and* bottom of the loom. Be careful not to pull the woof too tight to create a "pinched-in look." A pattern can still be created as described below.

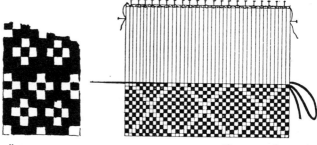

Small square pattern   Flower garden

PATTERN. The ordinary weave is over one, under one, but it is possible to achieve more varied patterns on this simple loom. You will need graph paper to work out your design. If your warp is a light color and your woof is dark (they could be any arrangement or all one color), you will fill in dark squares on your graph paper for the threads you wanted carried over. The patterns in the illustration are some traditional ones. Each square represents one thread. Try working out some designs of your own on paper and when one pleases you, make it up into fabric.

Finger weaving

Finger weaving is an art given to us by the Indians. Similar techniques seem to have been developed by tribes all over our country. The technique produces a very handsome belt or bookmark.

You will need: heavy weights of yarn (Germantown, knitting worsted, tapestry, or peasant yarns) and a pencil or short stick slightly longer than the width of the finished object. Fast-color cotton yarns such as rug fillers are also suitable. The number of strands of yarn depends upon the width desired. About 62 yarns make a 3-inch belt. The length is determined by the waist measure plus the amount needed for a knot, plus the length desired for sash ends and fringe.

Cut the desired number of colored yarns. For a beginning project, two or three colors are enough. There are many pattern possibilities, but for the beginner, we have included two of the less complicated ones. The yarns are tied on a narrow stick or pencil with enough left for a fringe. The weaving is always worked with the yarns on the stick. Tie the top strands together and tack the weaving on something just below eye level.

FOR THE DIAGONAL STRIPE, arrange even number of yarns on the stick in any pleasing color arrangement of stripes. Take the strand on the left and weave it over and under until it comes to the far right. Proceed always from the left and always start with a weave over. Remember always to weave the previously woven strand back in. If you keep it separated from the other strands until you

Setting up loom   Diagonal stripe   Chevron stripe

come across with the next strand, it is easier to keep straight. When you stop work, you can keep your belt from getting tangled if you tie all the strands together except the last woven strand. Keep your work even, taut, and firm but do not pull each thread too tight.

FOR THE CHEVRON STRIPE arrange an equal number of strands of each color on each side of the center of the stick to total to an even number. For example, starting from left to right there may be 10 navy, 15 mauve, 5 pale blue-green; 5 pale blue-green, 15 mauve, 10 navy. Start weaving with the first thread left of center and weave over, under, to the far right. Then take the first thread right of center and weave over and under to the far left. Continue weaving in this manner until the belt is complete. When weaving, it is important to keep the center division, so that you can always locate your weaving strand.

Tapestry weaving

After you have tried some of the more elementary steps in weaving, you may want to try working out a picture or more elaborate design in what is known as tapestry weaving. With this method you can make such things as a picture for the wall, a purse or knitting bag, pillow top, or several squares can be sewed together to make a rug. You can also use it in connection with another project such as one of those illustrated on pages 99-100.

A satisfactory frame can be made from the end of an orange crate with the sunken section removed; from a cigar box or picture frame. The frame should be as nearly square as possible and should be well sandpapered and smooth. Hammer an uneven number of nails at one end about ½ inch apart. Thread the loom with a sturdy warp (carpet warp or string). Tie the warp around the first nail, bring it down to the right of the nail, around the frame and back up to the same nail, loop it around the first nail and take it to the right of the second nail. Continue until all threads are on the nails. Bringing the warp around the whole loom in order to keep the nails from dropping out and to keep the warp threads taut. If you would rather, you can also place nails at the bottom edge and thread only the front side of the loom. The warp must be kept tight. When you are ready to weave, tie the warp tightly around the last nail.

All that has been said in this book about good design or taste applies equally well here. Plan your design on a sheet of paper the size of the inside of the frame. The finished work will be about ¾ of an inch smaller. In this kind of weaving, remember all lines must be horizontal, vertical, or diagonal. Cutting paper is an excellent way to create a design. Fold a piece of paper in half, cut the design, and you will have a bisymmetric pattern.

The first design should be simple, so make it in one color and the background in another. Slip this paper behind the warp threads—the back threads will hold it in place. Some people prefer to weave the design first and

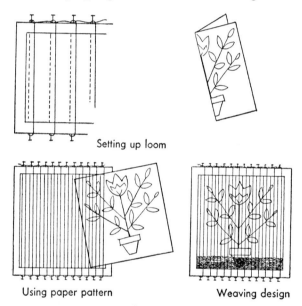

Setting up loom

Using paper pattern   Weaving design

the background later, but it will be more even if the work is woven row by row. You should have about eight rows of background above and below the pattern part of the picture. Unevenness is the hardest thing for the beginner to overcome. Avoid pulling the threads too tightly in spots and keep the warp thread perfectly parallel.

After you have tried the one-color design, you can experiment with more colors. Each color must have its own needle and the background color usually needs two, one for each side so that you do not have to carry threads for a long space over the back of the design. Use a small comb to push the rows close together. Where two colors come together, the two woof threads must lap over the same warp thread to avoid holes in the work.

Other methods

Other types of looms and weaving that you may like are shown on page 96. There is the Tee Dee loom for weaving narrow objects, such as belts or bookmarks. The loom can

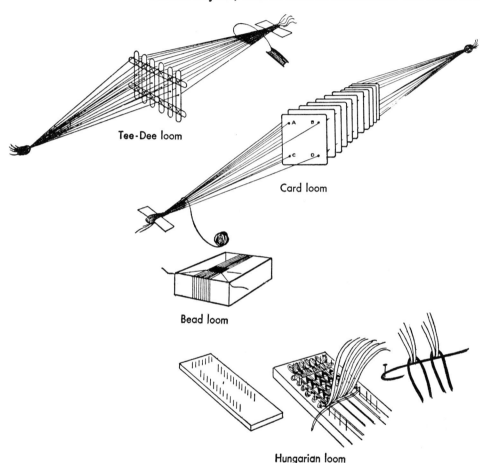

Tee-Dee loom

Card loom

Bead loom

Hungarian loom

be made from tongue depressors. Egyptian card weaving may look difficult from the illustration but it is actually quite simple and produces a very lovely belt. Hungarian weaving produces a belt with a loose-woven chevron design. The Indian bead loom is another interesting type of weaving to work out belts, bookmarks, fobs, etc. See the Bibliography for books on these types of weaving.

96

DECORATING FABRIC

Textile painting

If you and the troop are interested in textile painting, first read the chapter on prints which explains the techniques involved in making block prints, stencils, and silk screen designs. The processes are the same except that when printing on fabric you always use a permanent textile paint or an oil base printing ink. Or you can paint the design freehand right on the material.

Again the design must be adapted to the use. What is suitable for a square dance skirt may not be for place mats. If you are working on lengths of fabric you will need in addition to the supplies listed under the prints, tailor's chalk and a yardstick for marking the fabric, and some old pieces of muslin or sheeting to use to test patterns.

HINTS. If you are doing a repeat pattern, use the tailor's chalk and yardstick to mark the guide lines for placement of stencil, block or screen.

Mix all paints at one time to avoid a spotty look from different batches of paint. If you mix your inks on a piece of glass with a sheet of white paper under it, the colors will be more true.

Place a padding of newspapers on the floor for block prints, on a table for stencil and silk screen. Place the fabric on top. Print on a piece of test fabric first. Then on your fabric.

If you are doing a repeat design on a stencil or silk screen, place the design in every other space and then go back and fill it. This helps prevent smearing the ink.

Let the articles dry for at least twenty-four hours, then press on the wrong side with a medium hot iron.

Wash articles that have been decorated with printing in lukewarm water and mild soap, rinse well, hang straight and right side out to dry. Iron on wrong side.

Embroidery

For many years, part of the education of young women was to learn to embroider fine designs with a needle. This is no longer true in this country, and perhaps girls are glad that they do not have to sit by the hour and do laboriously detailed samplers. Embroidery can be remarkably

97

uncreative and boring, yet with the same stitches, you can make a design of your own and a handsome article either for yourself to wear or for your home. The lack of good taste that is seen in some needlework departments is appalling. There seems to be much too great an attempt at realism in many of these patterns to produce anything worth while. You can, however, gain inspiration and source material in the library and museum. Look for English crewel embroidery, Scandinavian tapestries, peasant embroidery, Mexican and Oriental designs, and the work (seen in magazines) of the modern artists who have turned to embroidery as one of the fine arts. Some designs are not suitable for embroidery of course, but the person with an active imagination can see an interesting motif inspired from nature, from some types of embroidery, from a painted design on a box, or from a simple wood carving. Notice we said "inspired from" and not "copied from."

The materials you need will depend upon the object to be made or the design to be used. In general, however, you can use scraps of fabric, all kinds of yarn and embroidery floss, open-weave background materials such as burlap, or monk's cloth. Felt and tightly woven muslin are also useful for background fabrics. You need large, blunt

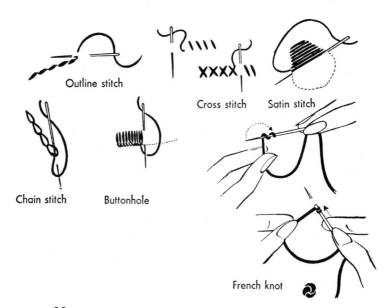

Outline stitch

Cross stitch   Satin stitch

Chain stitch   Buttonhole

French knot

needles (size 15-17) and can use string, cord, twine, and various decorative cords, as well as decorative beads, pearls, braid, etc.

The illustration opposite shows a few basic stitches. Practice on these before starting your adventure with the needle. Build up your repertoire of stitches gradually, rather than trying to accomplish all at once.

In teaching children to do creative embroidery sometimes it is best to let them use their imagination freely instead of teaching stitches. You will find they arrive at conventional stitches through their own experimentation.

You might start first with burlap and large stitches in just an abstract design. Then try working on a linen or Indian Head to enrich your wardrobe or surroundings. Try table mats, curtains, bedspread, wall hanging, or just a picture. Combine embroidery with other arts, in a pillow top, covering for a brick, cover of a box.

You can use appliqué effectively for wall hangings and pictures and use your stitches to create other pictures. You can make a stitch change character by using finer or coarser thread to create the desired effect. The same stitch might resemble a trellis, a fish net, or a spider web; worked close it might be a stone wall, raindrops, or just a geometric form. This art is difficult to set down because it is so individual and creative.

If inspiration comes hard to the girls, help them coordinate with something in their home or wardrobe. For example, a design from china or silver may be effective on place mats. Guide them to adapt rather than to reproduce exactly. Their own free designs are much better than slavish reproduction.

NEEDLEPOINT

The sad thing about this beautiful old art is much the same as embroidery. Nowadays, too much needlepoint is done by merely filling in the background of someone else's design. If the child is encouraged to do this repetition, she loses her potential for creating her own ideas. It takes all the joy of creating out of the work and merely reduces it to a mechanical pushing of a needle. With the various needlepoint stitches, pictured on page 100, you can create something satisfying, personal, and beautiful. You can buy the needlepoint backing by the yard and the only other

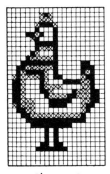

Planning Design

Continental stitch

Half-cross or tapestry stitch

materials needed are yarn, a blunt needle, and imagination. The possibilities are tremendous.

Start on a small piece first. Then you can decide whether the technique is to your liking and you won't be faced with a big project you must finish if you don't want to. Take a 4-inch square of needlepoint mesh—10 squares to the inch. Use this square merely for experimentation or, if you like it, use it as a pocket on a plain smock, framed as a little picture, as an inset on a purse, book end, or book cover.

Start with one simple motif, and sketch it to size planning for 5 to 8 rows of border around the central motif. You may want to use just your sketch as a guide and work into the backing without any detailed design. However, for larger and more intricate motifs you will need a design planned on graph paper with colored pencils. Keep the first design limited to a few colors, one or two for the motif and one color for the background. The illustration shows how you transfer the sketch to the graph paper as the guide for your needlepoint stitches. Try the regular needlepoint stitch first, before you attempt the more intricate ones. Work the motif first, then fill in the background. Refer to books in the Bibliography for more stitches and techniques, and look in your library and museums for inspiration.

Here are a few general hints for finishing and lining your work which apply to whatever you make.

BLOCKING. Cover an old table or board with brown paper, mark the size of the canvas on this, being sure the corners are square. Place needlepoint right side down over the guide, fasten with thumbtacks about ¾ of an inch apart along the edge of the canvas. Wet with cold water and let dry. If piece was too badly out of line to straighten it the first time, repeat the blocking process.

FINISHING. If you are using your needlepoint as a chair seat or for a stool, do not cut off any of the canvas. On all other pieces cut off all but ⅜ inch after blocking. Fold the excess to the back, clipping at corners and curves to make it lie flat, and catch stitch to the back. Some pieces, like luggage rack straps, eyeglass cases, etc., need stiffening with one or more layers of tailor's canvas stitched together. Cut these pieces ⅛ inch smaller than the needlepoint, and catch stitch to the back. For lining, cut a piece

100

¾ inch larger than the needlepoint. Turn under the seam allowance, clip corners and curves, and slip stitch to the back. Some articles are improved if a small cord is sewed along the edge between the needlepoint and the lining. You can buy this cord or make it by twisting together several strands of the wool yarn.

HOOKED RUGS

Rug hooking, like the arts mentioned earlier, is one of the old arts that is now found in presketched, predesigned, and almost preworked form in the stores today. It is not this type of hooked rug discussed here, but rather that which is designed and executed from the beginning, with a special room or purpose in mind.

You will need: simple tools and yarn to start with. Then when you have progressed to more advanced projects, you can acquire some of the better hooking tools and fabric. We have listed all the tools among which you may choose, depending on your project.

RUG BASE. Burlap is the traditional rug base and is cheapest; you can also use evenly woven cotton such as monk's cloth. Cotton rug base called warp cloth and linen rug base are more expensive and longer lasting.

SURFACE MATERIALS. Wool, cotton, silk, and felt are all usable, but the best is wool. It takes a dye better and doesn't show soil as quickly. You may use strips of old materials—wool suits, dresses, denim trousers, or you may buy bundles of already cut strips. Avoid fabrics that fray easily. Yarn is also used but it is more expensive for large rugs. Old washed wools give best soft colors.

You need about ½ pound of material for each square foot of rug.

TOOLS. Shears, cloth strippers, or cutters. The material must be cut either by hand or by a mechanical cutter sold in needlework stores. Usually strips are cut about ¼ inch wide—lightweight fabrics are cut wider, heavier fabrics cut narrower. Avoid seams in cutting, do not join the strips.

FRAME. Make a frame slightly larger than your rug with four strips of wood 2 x 3 inches, four clamps, thumbtacks, and, if you wish, several long shoelaces or yards of cord to lace burlap to frame. A frame is not necessary for all hooked rugs, especially the small projects the girls would start with.

HOOKERS. Shuttle hooker or Bluenose hooker (can be adjusted for height of loop, produces loops close together). These tools hook from the back. Hand hook and crochet hook are used from front (holding fabric with left hand and pulling up through rug base with tool held in right hand). A punch needle is used from back of the rug but serves the same purposes as the hand hooker and crochet hook.

RUG BACKING. This is a liquid to seal hooking (obtainable at notion counters).

For the first design try something small, perhaps a rectangle design to fit on a brick. Measure the top of the brick and cut the rug backing about 2 inches larger all around. The brick can be covered with muslin or cotton batting and then with felt, burlap, or other sturdy material, and when the hooked piece is put on top, the brick is usable as a doorstop, book end, or weight for holding paper patterns while cutting. A small project is suggested first, so that the beginner will not be discouraged by having committed herself to a large work. For such a small project you could use rug yarn or fabric cut in narrow widths and a medium-sized rug hook, working from the front. Keep the first design simple—geometric pattern, stripe, or a single motif. You do not need a frame for such a small project.

Cut the rug base to size, prepare the strips by cutting. Choose the colors you like, spread the strips out on the couch or floor and arrange them to give the desired effects. Plan a sketch of the rug you wish to make, and sketch it on the burlap base with crayon. It is easier if you clip a piece of the color swatch alongside the sketch to help remind you of the color plan, but don't be afraid to change as you go along. Experiment on a scrap with different textures such as a high loop, low loop, cut loop, and uncut loop, and plan a nice variety. Give variety of only one

kind at a time—that is color, or texture—not both at the same time.

Now you are ready to begin hooking. This is hooking with rug hooker or crochet hook. Hold the yarn or strip in the left hand, push the needle into the backing with the right hand, and pull the strip through to a loop about ¼ inch high; continue making your loops in this way. Don't worry if at first your loops are uneven. It takes practice to make even loops. Always end a strip by pulling through to the front and cutting off even with the loops. If your loops are uneven, you may want to trim them on this first project. Do the details first, and fill in the background last. With a fine burlap, wools cut narrow, and a fine rug hook you can also make beautiful pictures.

It is easier to work a large rug on a frame because you can see the part you are working on in relation to the whole. However, a frame is not necessary. When you are ready to start a large project, you will probably want to try one of the mechanical rug hookers. Directions for these come with the tool. They will make your hooking go faster.

Gain inspiration for your rugs from museums where you can find lovely old designs, and from exhibits where modern artists have used their art in hooked rugs. You will see that some modern designers use such things as squares of fur and other interesting textures for their rugs. You might like to experiment with such things too. Plan your design to go with the color scheme and furniture in the room you are planning it for. Very interesting effects can be obtained by using architectural inspiration. The illustrations show sketches for hooked rugs but unfortunately cannot show the soft color and texture that is so beautiful.

FINISHING. After the design is finished, dampen the rug with a cloth or sponge. Place the rug face down on several layers of brown paper or newspaper covered with brown paper and walk on it. Let it dry. A small piece can be pressed on the back using a damp muslin cloth and hot iron. Turn in the rug backing and hem, sew a binding around the edge if desired. Paint rug backing on the back to hold loops firmly in position and to prevent rug from slipping. Let rug dry for two days before using. If you do not want to paint on the solution, line the rug with burlap.

103

ANSWERS TO QUIZ ON PAGE 6

1b. This cup and saucer is better design because of proportion, scale, and function. The cup is in better proportion to the saucer and the handle is of pleasing shape and easy to hold.

2b. This lamp is better design because it is all lamp, well suited to its purpose. The shade is in good proportion to its base. Compare the length of shade *a* to its base—it is practically equal. Notice too, how much wider the circle of light lamp *b* will allow. Lamp *b* attempts to emulate an antique vase with a too small shade on top.

3b. Chest *b* is better design essentially because of harmony, proportion, and honesty. It allows the beauty of the wood to attain the prominence. Good design does not depend on whether a piece is traditional or modern. Both these chests are an old design. Chest *b* is a Shaker blanket chest, lovingly made by people who created usefulness without unnecessary details and thus achieved beauty. Chest *a* is a copy of ornateness stemming from another era, and is therefore inappropriate to restful simple interiors. Harmony is hurt by its too many curves and Pennsylvania Dutch designs painted in an inappropriate setting.

4b. This chair is better design because of simplicity, function, harmony, and balance. Its lines are restful, quiet, comfortable as is befitting a chair.

Chair *a* is in unhappy proportion. The top seems heavy for the small base, the arms look too straight and stiff for comfort. The modern looking fabric is most inappropriate for the period of the chair.

Although we have not mentioned color and texture, these elements would be considered. In judging good design, we should always consider its use: all good design is useful. Good design makes good use of materials, its various parts are related in shape, and color and texture are related to the whole design.

104